Matriarchs and Mean Girls and Shamans Oh My...!!

MATRIARCHS
AND MEAN GIRLS
AND SHAMANS
OH MY...!!

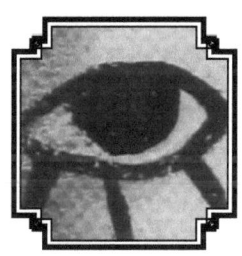

WALTER GUERRA OSTOLAZA

TWO ROOMS PRESS
SAN FRANCISCO

Two Rooms Press
1326 16th Avenue
San Francisco, California 94122
TRPress@mac.com

Printed in the U.S.
First Edition, 2013

Cover design by Walter Guerra Ostolaza
Book design by Walter Guerra Ostolaza
and Jonathan Aaberg
This book was typset in Trajan Pro and Palatino.

Matriarchs and Mean Girls and Shamans Oh My...!!
ISBN-13: 978-0-9847369-4-2

To my mother, whose tales were the inspiration for this book
and to my sister Nelly, the Matriarch of my family in the present.
Love you so much.

CONTENTS

Publisher's Foreword

2012 and 2013 have proven to be very productive and busy years for Walter Guerra Ostolaza. Following successful exhibits of what came to be known as his *Allegories* series, his decision to paint his enigmatic Aunt Clotilde seemed to pull back the curtain to reveal a series already gestating in his subconscious—*Matriarchs*.

This series with its stylistic shift toward paintings with cubist inflections and explicit conception as a series seemed to arrive fully formed. Loosely speaking the paintings are based on women in the ancestry of the artist, but they also serve as repositories of different facets of archetypal female power (eg. Maria Magdalena, Susana) as well as vulnerability (eg. Clotilde, The Two Teresas).

On this side of life these women were separated by years and generations. On the other side, as the artist seems to suggest, they are more connected, more directly linked to each other, perhaps even having an afterlife coffee klatch from which they observe and comment on the dramas of the living.

As if to call for its opposite, or at any rate orthogonal, dimension of female power, *Matriarchs* opened a portal to the series with its deceptively diminutive title—*Mean Girls*. Now, downplaying the legacy of Lucrezia Borgia and compounding the matter by using the diminutive "girls" seems to be playing with fire. (I suppose the corresponding test would be a thought experiment revolving around reactions to a series entitled "Bad Boys" including portraits ranging from Adolf Hitler to Rasputin).

One possible interpretation could be that the diminutive title *"Mean Girls"* signifies the problem, *a la* patriarchal repression and a backlash. I think a richer landscape emerges if we consider the possibility that if there are

viii

Palabras del Editor

2012 y 2013 han sido años de mucha actividad y productividad para Walter Guerra Ostolaza. Después de la exitosa exhibición de la serie llamada *Alegorías,* su decisión de pintar a su enigmática tía Clotilde aparentemente abrió la cortina para revelar una serie que estaba desde ya formándose en su subconsciente—*Matriarcas.*

Esta serie con su cambio estilístico hacia una pintura con influencia cubista y concebida como un con junto que arriba completamente formado en apariencia. Hablando a la ligera, las pinturas están basadas en las mujeres del pasado familiar del artista, pero ellas sirven además como representantes de los arquetipos del poder femenino (ej. María Magdalena, Susana) asi como de vulnerabilidad (ej. Clotilde, Las Dos Teresas).

Por un lado, estas mujeres estaban separadas por años y generaciones. Por otro lado, como el artista parece sugerir, ellas están más conectadas, más directamente ligadas entre sí, posiblemente compartiendo una taza de café desde el más allá desde donde observan y comentan los dramas de los vivos.

Como si llamada por la opuesta o, en cualquier caso, ortogonal dimensión del poder femenino, *Matriarcas* abre un portal para otra serie con un engañoso título diminutivo—*Niñas Malas.* Ahora, minimizar el legado de Lucrecia Borgia y agravar el asunto usando el diminutivo de "niñas" es, aparentemente, jugar con fuego. (Supongo que el experimento correspondiente seria intentar ver las reacciones frente a una serie llamada "Chicos Malos" que incluya personajes como Adolfo Hitler o Rasputín).

Una posible interpretación podría ser que el título diminutivo de *Niñas Malas* represente una respuesta al problema de la represión patriarcal y una revancha contra esta. Yo pienso

variations of archetypal power of the male and female variety (and of that precious but rare territory between them) then how do those archetypes interact and express positively and negatively whether in actual persons or cultural representations. Betty Crocker or Bonnie Parker? Hello Dolly or Mata Hari?

Simpler patriarchal assumptions crack open to reveal the tapestry of history embroidered with virtue and excess and violence and injury—more than enough for all—and on its reverse the broken threads and unexpected crossings that hold it all together. In *Mean Girls*, the artist has certainly pulled together an unexpected assembly from the front of the tapestry, and presented the thoughtful among us with some questions that might require us to peer behind the curtain. The rest is conjecture.

After all the energy summoned by the two series *Matriarchs* and *Mean Girls*—"The Ladies" as we have casually come to describe them—the artist needed a small adjunct series to back away a bit, to calm, and to give perspective. This need produced the series *Shamans*—four paintings, not specific persons, but supportive archetypal forces embedded in forms of the natural world and loosely associated with High Desert Native American Pomo and Mojave mythologies.

These paintings are preliminary to the artist's brief residency in the High Desert in the area near Joshua Tree, California—a place to retreat and create before taking "The Ladies" on the road to their premiere in New London, Connecticut in July, 2013.

Now that will be quite a road trip. Watch Out!

J.A.

que aparece una vasta cantidad de posibilidades si consideramos la variedad de arquetipos de poder masculino y femenino (y aquel territorio raro, pero precioso entre ellos) y como aquellos arquetipos interactúan y se expresan positiva o negativamente en personas reales o representaciones culturales. ¿Betty Crocker o Bonnie Parker? ¿Hello Dolly o Mata Hari?

Las simples suposiciones patriarcales se abren para revelar la tapicería de historias bordadas con virtudes, excesos y violencia—más que suficiente de esto—y sus hilos rasgados y extrañamente cruzados que mantienen todo esto unido. En *Chicas Malas*, el artista ha creado un conjunto inesperado desde el frente de esta tapicería, y nos ha hecho pensar en algunas preguntas que requieren que veamos detrás de esta cortina. El resto son suposiciones.

Después de toda la energía puesta en las series *Matriarcas* y *Chicas Malas* -"Las Damas" como las describimos familiarmente- el artista necesitaba trabajar una pequeña serie que le permitiera tomar cierta distancia, calmarse y recuperar perspectiva. Esta necesidad produjo la serie *Shamanes* - cuatro pinturas, no personas específicas, pero arquetipos de las fuerzas que se sostienen en as formas del mundo natural y libremente asociadas con las mitologias de los Nativos Pomo y Mojave del Desierto Alto de California.

Estas pinturas son el preludio a una breve residencia del artista en el Desierto Alto en el área cercana al Joshua Tree, California—un lugar donde retirarse y crear antes de llevar a "Las Damas" a su primera presentación pública en New London, Connecticut en Julio del 2013.

Ese va a ser un viaje interesante. !Estén atentos!

Traducción W.G.O.

PREFACE
MATRIARCHS AND MEAN GIRLS AND SHAMANS OH MY...!!

This book presents the art pieces I have worked on in the last ten years, since my arrival in the United States until the present day, with particular focus on the pieces that I have made in the period between 2011 and 2013, when I, in some way, decided to pay tribute to the legacy which my mother gave me through the stories she told me when I was a child, the books that she allowed me to read in my teenage days, and the values that she instilled in me throughout my life.

I was opposed for a long time to the painting of series. I preferred painting individual pieces that represented my mood and my vision of the reality around me at the moment of conceiving the art piece. This changed when I started painting *Matriarchs*. They differentiate themselves from traditional painting series in that each of them is painted in a different format, and some of them in different styles, but they have in common the fact that they are my representation of the female members of my family. I didn't meet all of them because many of them were already deceased by the time when I was born, but my mother, as keeper of their stories, transmitted that legacy to me through bedtime stories she told me in my childhood. In those stories I learned of the love and care that these women had for the family, as well as the tragedies of their lives, and of the ways in which they either overcame or succumbed to the challenges that life presented to them.

In the case of *Mean Girls*, I decided to challenge myself to make a series that would in some way be more conventional. All of them are painted in canvases of the same size, forcing me to be more consistent in the way they

X

PREFACIO
MATRIARCAS Y CHICAS MALAS Y SHAMANES OH MI...!!

Este libro presenta los trabajos artísticos en los que he trabajado durante los últimos diez años, desde mi llegada a los Estados Unidos hasta la fecha, enfocándome, especialmente, en el período comprendido entre los años 2011 y 2013, cuando, de cierta manera, decidí pagar tributo al legado que mi madre me dió a través de las historias que me contaba cuando era niño, los libros que me permitió leer durante mi adolescencia, y los valores que ella ha inspirado en mi durante toda mi vida.

Por mucho tiempo yo me opuse a la pintura de series. Yo prefería pintar piezas individuales que representaran mi estado de ánimo y mi visión de la realidad en el momento de concepción del trabajo artístico. Eso cambió cuando comencé a pintar las *Matriarcas*. Ellas se diferencian de las series de pinturas tradicionales en de que cada una de ellas está pintada en diferentes formatos, y, algunas de ellas en diferentes estilos, pero tienen en común el hecho de que son mi representación de los miembros femeninos de mi familia. Yo no conocí a todas ellas, porque muchas de ellas ya habían fallecido cuando yo nací, pero mi madre, como guardiana de sus historias, me transmitió ese legado en la forma de historias que me contaba para dormir en la época de mi niñez. En esas historias yo pude conocer el amor y cuidado que estas mujeres pusieron en la familia, las tragedias de sus vidas, así como el modo como ellas superaron o sucumbieron a los retos que la vida les presentó.

En el caso de las *Chicas Malas*, decidí desafiarme a mí mismo y hacer una serie que fuera de algún modo más convencional. Todas ellas están pintadas en lienzos de las mismas dimensiones, forzándome a ser más consistente

are painted. They represent historical characters from stories that my mother also told me in my early adolescence, and from books I used to read and discuss with her. They were the villains in all these stories of drama, crime, and betrayal. These were women who were capable of anything in pursuing their ambition to get or keep power, or who were simply used as sexual bait by others in order to further their own ambitions.

The series *Shamans*, by contrast, comes from a more introspective search into the totemic beliefs of the Native American traditions, especially from the area of the High Desert of California. The animals, landscape and native people of the area form a unity that is incomparable. The power of the Shaman comes from the power that the earth gives to him or her. It is a power gained from the spiritual connection through the roots that link the Shaman with their natural surroundings. Each rock, animal or plant has a spirit and it is the mission of the Shaman to keep the connection between his/her people and these spirits in harmony and balance. These paintings presented a different kind of challenge for me because the size in which they are painted was larger than the sizes I usually paint, and the subject of the paintings was something new for me.

In the section *"Oh My…!!"* I have included the paintings I call *Allegories*. These are pieces that in some way are my personal views of society and its values. The rest of the pieces are a diversity of paintings representing my own feelings and desires.

W.G.O.

en la forma como ellas están pintadas. Ellas representan personajes reales de historias que mi madre me contaba durante mi adolescencia temprana, y de libros que yo leía y discutía con ella. Ellas eran las villanas de esas historias de drama, crimen y traición. Eran mujeres capaces de todo en busca de satisfacer sus ambiciones de conseguir o mantener el poder, o quienes simplemente fueron usadas como carnada sexual por otros más poderosos o ambiciosos.

La serie de los *Shamanes*, en contraste, viene de una búsqueda más introspectiva de las creencias totémicas dentro de las tradiciones nativas de América, especialmente en el área del Desierto Alto de California. Los animales, paisaje y gente nativa del área forman una unidad que es incomparable. El poder del Shaman viene del poder que la tierra le otorga. Es un poder ganado a través de la conección espiritual con las raíces que conectan al Shaman con su entorno natural. Cada roca, animal o planta tiene un espíritu y la misión del Shaman es mantener la conección entre su gente y estos espíritus en armonía y balance. Estas pinturas representaron un desafío diferente por las dimensiones en las que fueron pintadas, que son mayores a las dimensiones en las que yo pinto generalmente, y el sujeto de las pinturas que era algo nuevo para mí.

En la sección llamada *"Oh Mi...!!"* he incluido las pinturas llamadas *Alegorías*. Estos trabajos son de cierta manera mi visión personal de la sociedad y sus valores. El resto de las piezas son trabajos que representan mis sentimientos y deseos.

W.G.O.

xi

The Artist

Walter Guerra Ostolaza

I was born in Lima Peru. At age 16 I began my studies in the National School of Fine Arts in Lima, Peru, and continued my studies in the Inter American Seminary for the Preservation of the National Heritage organized by the American States Organization (ASO) and the Andrés Bello Agreement in the City of Cusco, where I received my certification as Specialist in Colonial painting conservation.

I worked for 13 years in the preservation of the colonial patrimony of my country, in the cities of Lima, Cusco, Huamanga and Cajamarca. As additional work, I designed the costumes and sets for several theatre plays and ballets in my country. I have participated in many exhibitions in Lima, Cusco, and San Francisco, where I have been living since 2002. I have had two individual shows in 2011 and 2012 in San Francisco. I will be artist-in-residence for one month in New London, Connecticut, starting July 3, 2013, where I also will have an exhibition of my paintings and will be teaching a class to teenage students during their summer camp.

My artwork is in diverse private collections in Lima, San Miguel de Piura (Peru), San Francisco, Oakland (California), New York, Barcelona, Madrid, Santiago de Cuba, Santa Cruz (Bolivia), Bauru (Brazil), and Santo Domingo (Dominican Republic). My artwork has also been featured in the book *Nuestras Mil Caras, Latino Sexual Rebellion* published by Project La Familia, a collaboration between San Francisco State University, the San Francisco AIDS Foundation and the Universidad Autónoma de Zacatecas.

El Artista

Walter Guerra Ostolaza

Naci en Lima, Perú. A la edad de 16 comencé mis estudios en la Escuela Nacional de Bellas Artes en Lima, Perú, y los continué en el Seminario Inter Americano para la Preservación del Patrimonio Nacional, organizado por la Organización de Estados Americanos (OEA), el Instituto Nacional de Cultura y el Convenio Andrés Bello en la Ciudad de Cuzco, donde recibí mi certificación como Especialista en la Conservación de Pintura Colonial.

Trabajé por 13 años en la preservación del patrimonio cultural de mi país, en las ciudades de Lima, Cuzco, Huamanga y Cajamarca. He participado en diversas exposiciones en Lima, Cusco y San Francisco, donde he estado residiendo desde el año 2002. He tenido dos exposiciones individuales en San Francisco. A principios de Julio del 2013, voy a iniciar una residencia como artista por un mes en New London, Connecticut, donde, además de exhibir mis obras, voy a dictar una clase a un grupo de estudiantes adolescentes durante su campamento de verano.

Mis trabajos se encuentran en diversas colecciones privadas en Lima, San Miguel de Piura (Perú), San Francisco, Oakland (California), New York, Barcelona, Santiago de Ciuba, Santa Cruz (Bolivia), Baurú (Brasil) y Santo Domingo (Republica Dominicana). Mi trabajo ha sido ademas publicado en el libro *Nuestras Mil Caras, Latino Sexual Rebellions,* publicado por el Proyecto La Familia, una colaboración entre la Universidad Estatal de San Francisco, la Fundación contra el SIDA de San Francisco y la Universidad Autónoma de Zacatecas.

SELECTED EXHIBITIONS

2013   Catholic Charities Art Show, San Francisco.

2012   United in Hope, Workspace Gallery, San Francisco.

2012   Allegories, Latino Prevention Center, San Francisco.

2011   Erotic Art, Eros Lounge, San Francisco.

2011   The Identity Project, Hospitality House, San Francisco.

2010   Naked Men Sketch, Eros Lounge, San Francisco.

2010   Dias de Los Muertos, Oakland Museum of California.

2010   11 Men, 22 Eyes, Back the Painting Gallery, SOMA, San Francisco.

2009   Open Studio, San Francisco

2007   Personal Secrets, Public Spaces, SoMArts, San Francisco.

2005   (Un)Godly Bodies, SoMArts, San Francisco.

2005   Locos Peligrosos, Mission Cultural Center for Latino Arts, San Francisco.

2004   Trans-Cendences, SoMArts, San Francisco.

2004   Off the Wall, Continuum, San Francisco.

1990   Proyecto Identidad, ASPAP Gallery, Miraflores, Lima, Peru.

1990   Laboratorio Artístico, Pancho Fierro, Municipal Gallery, Lima, Peru.

1989   Nueve Noveles, El Greco Art Gallery, Lima, Peru.

1989   Nuevos Valores, El Greco Art Gallery, Lima, Peru.

1989   Promoción 1989, Alliance Française,Lima, Peru.

1987   New Generation, Cooperativa Santa Elisa, Lima, Peru.

1983   Art Exhibition, Municipality of Lince Art Gallery, Lima, Peru.

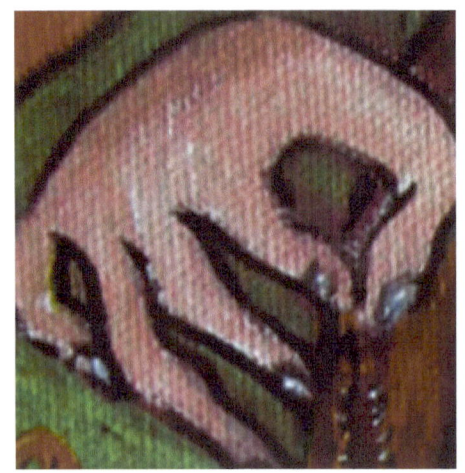

MATRIARCHS

Natividad
Woman with Grapes

Acrylic on canvas / Acrílico sobre lienzo
7 in x 9 in / 18 cm x 23 cm
2012

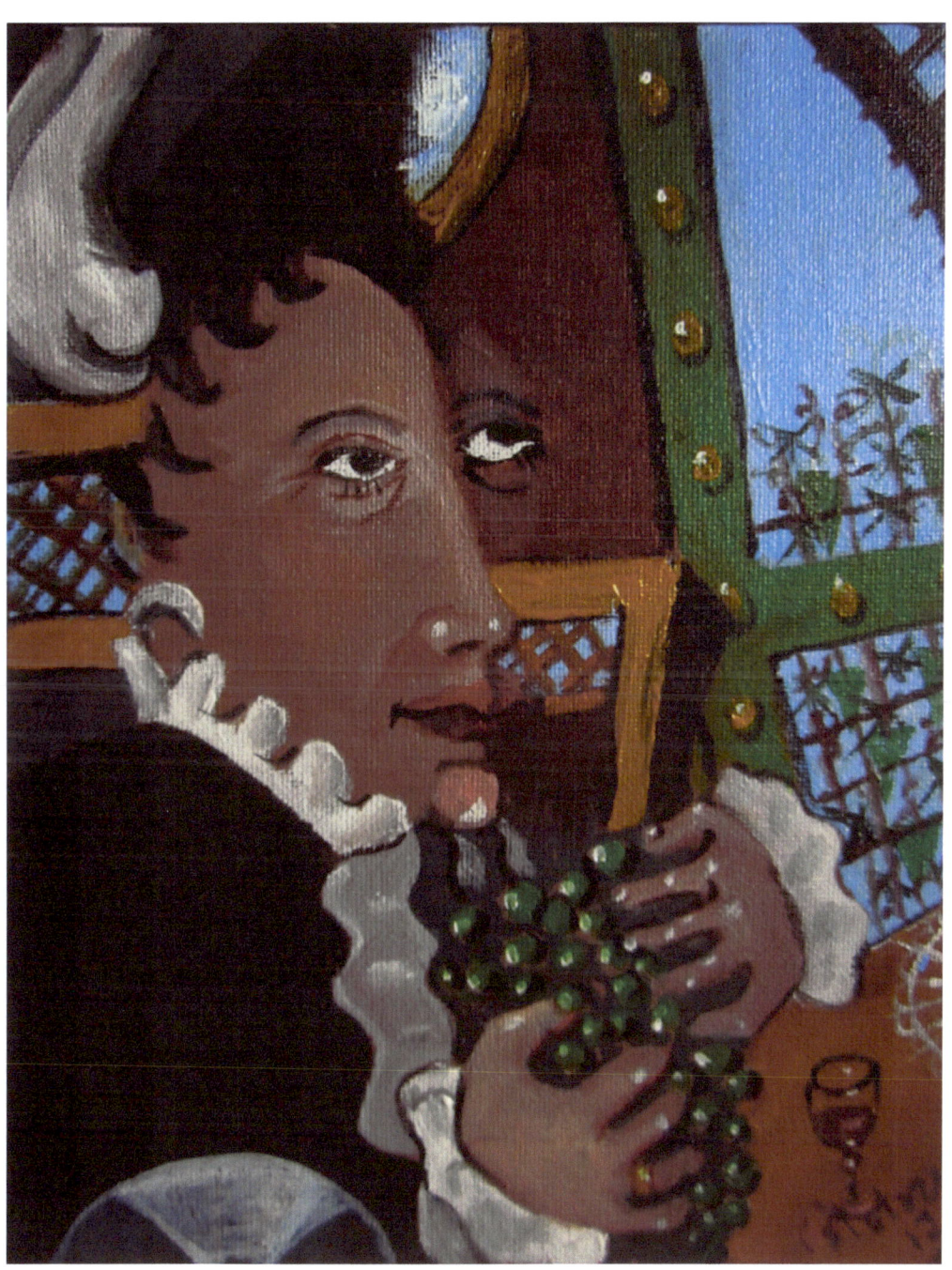

Margarita
Woman with Rosary

Acrylic on canvas / Acrílico sobre lienzo
8 in x 8 in / 20 cm x 20 cm
2012

4

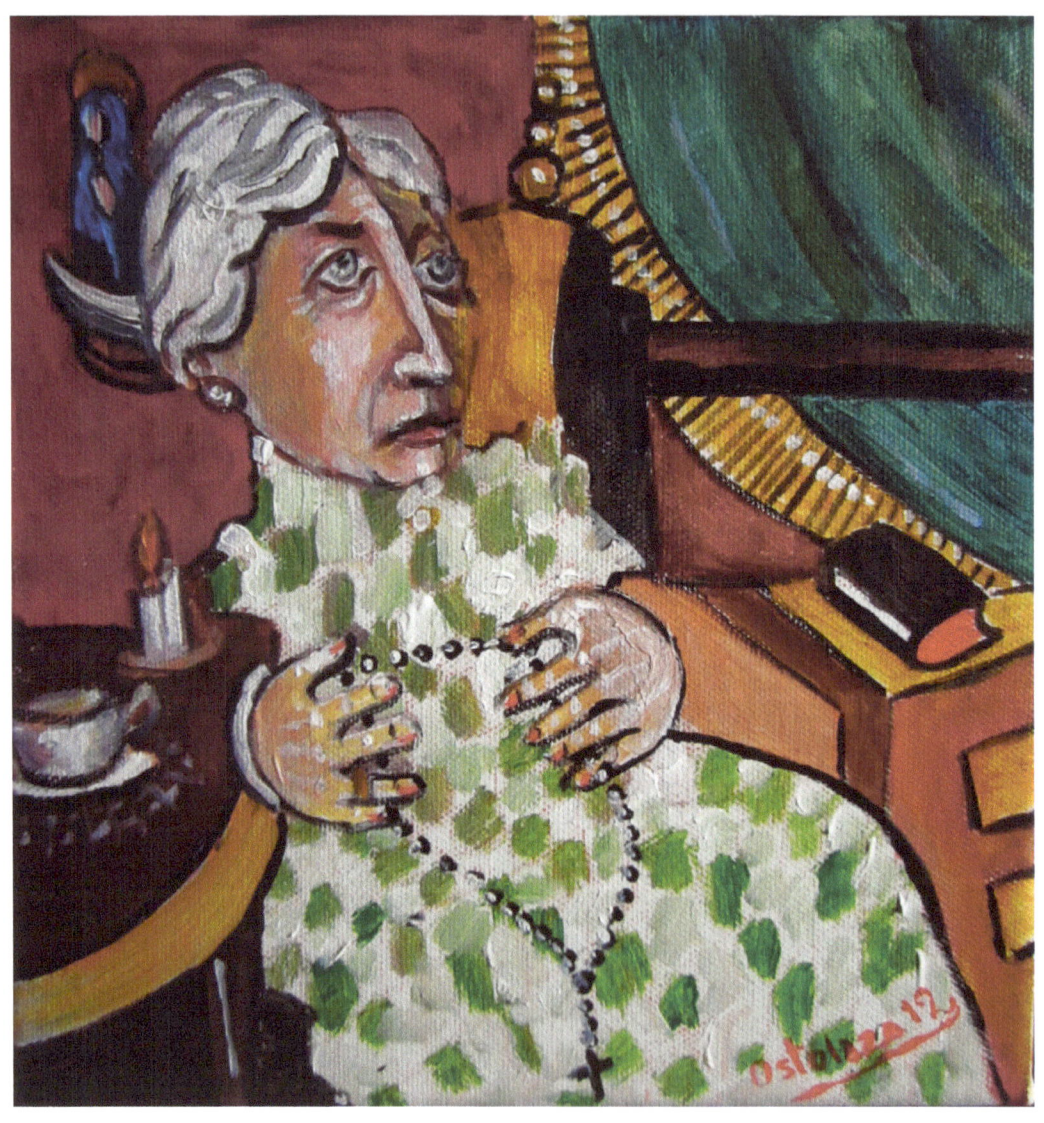

Maria Magdalena
Woman Throwing Jewels

Acrylic on canvas / Acrílico sobre lienzo
8 in x 10 in / 20 cm x 25 cm
2012

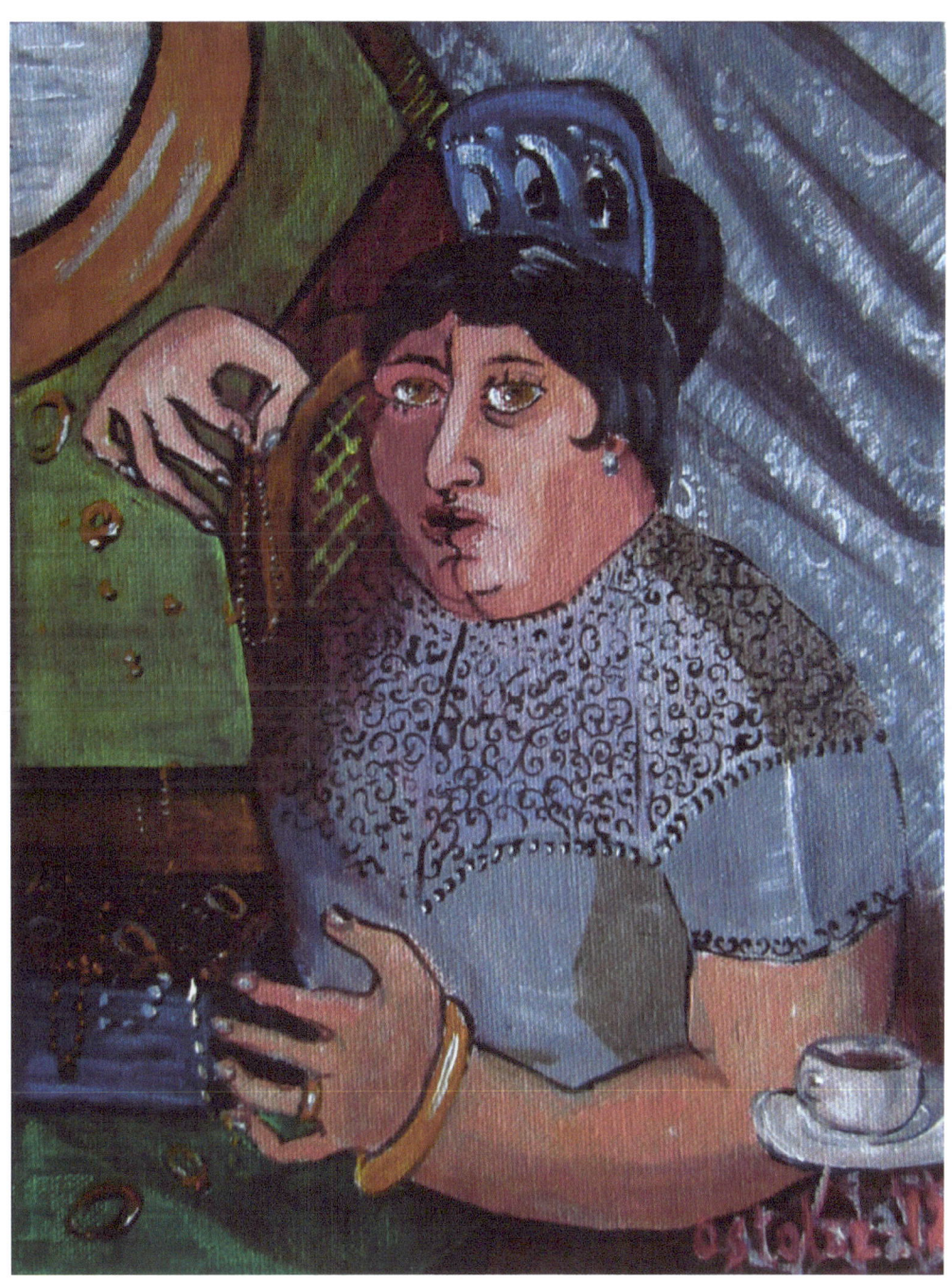

CLOTILDE
WOMAN BY THE WINDOW

Acrylic on canvas / Acrílico sobre lienzo
12 in x 12 in / 30 cm x 30 cm
2012

6

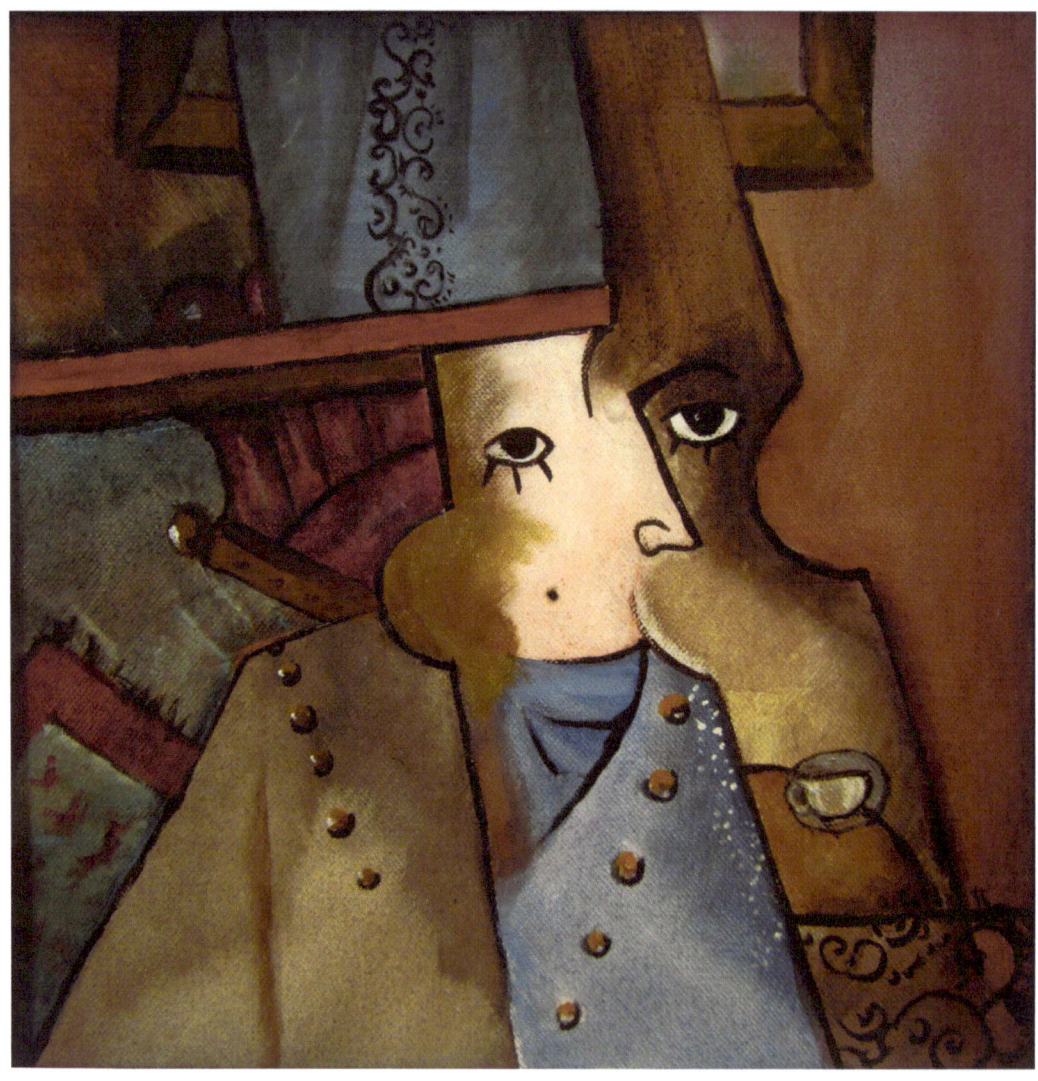

CRISTINA
WOMAN WITH FOX FUR

Acrylic on canvas / Acrílico sobre lienzo
9 in x 12 in / 23 cm x 30 cm
2012

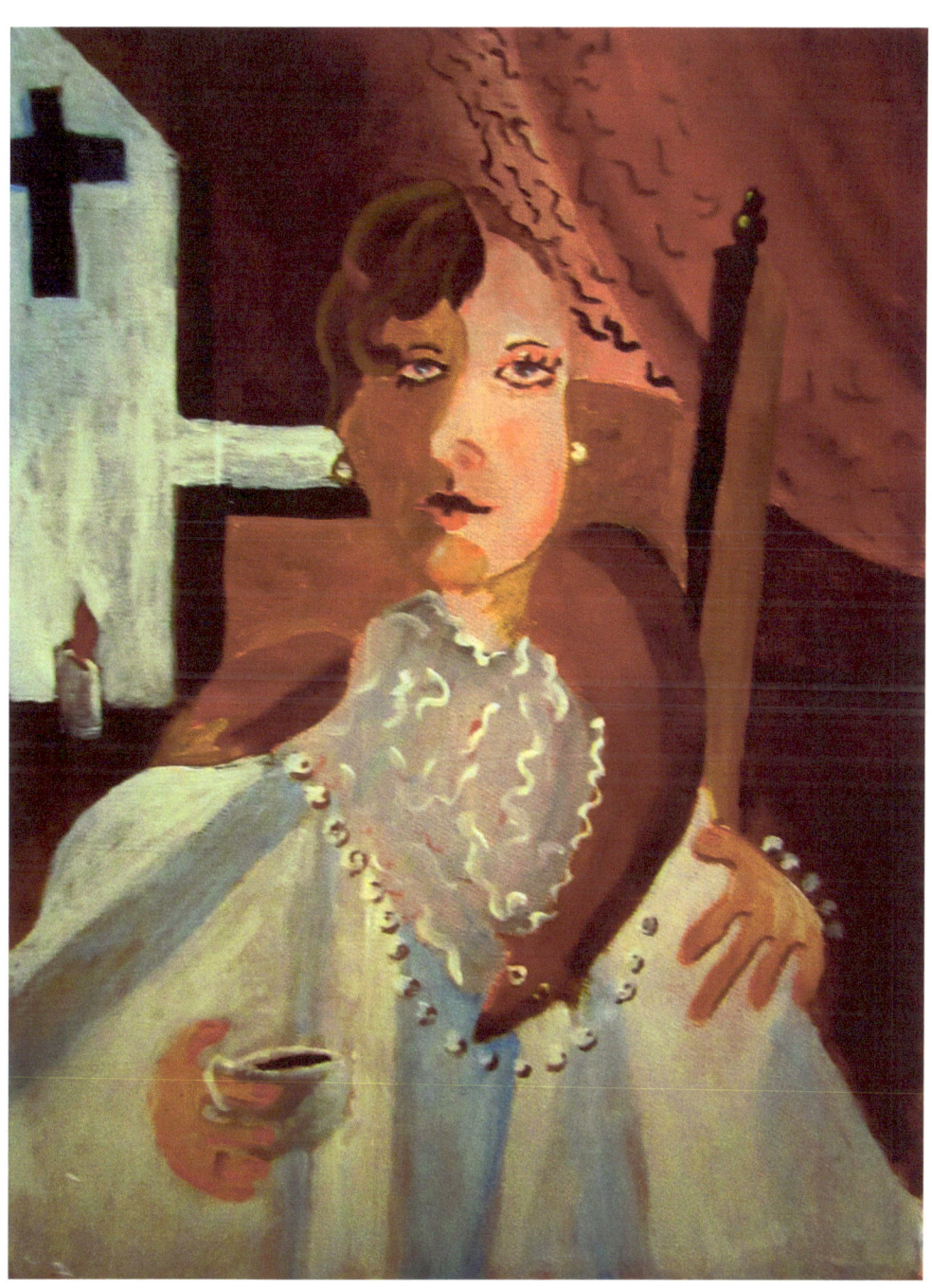

ELVIRA
PREGNANT WOMAN

Acrylic on canvas / Acrílico sobre lienzo
8 in x 10 in / 20 cm x 25 cm
2012

8

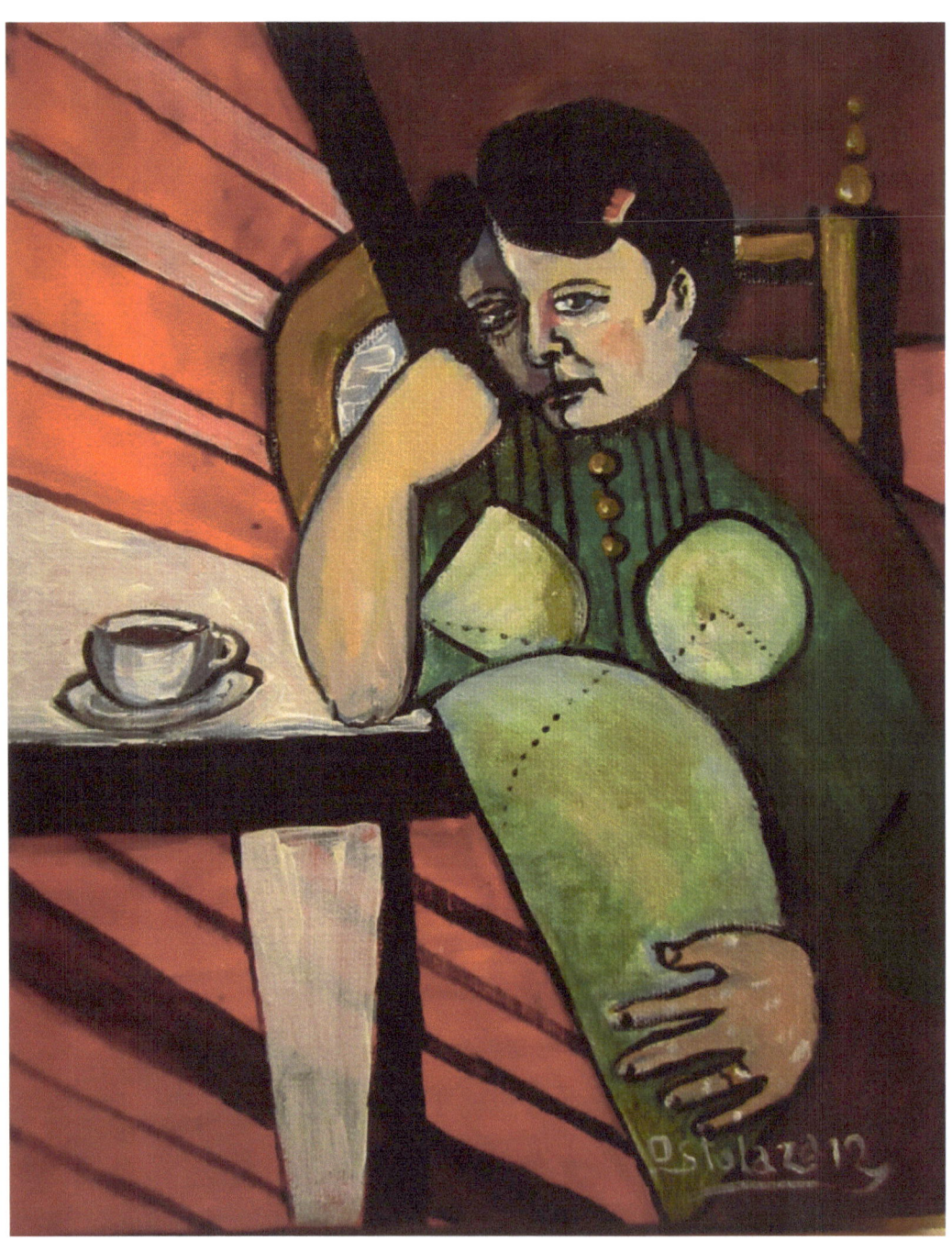

THE TWO TERESAS
MOTHER AND DAUGHTER

Acrylic on canvas / Acrílico sobre lienzo
8 in x 10 in / 20 cm x 25 cm
2012

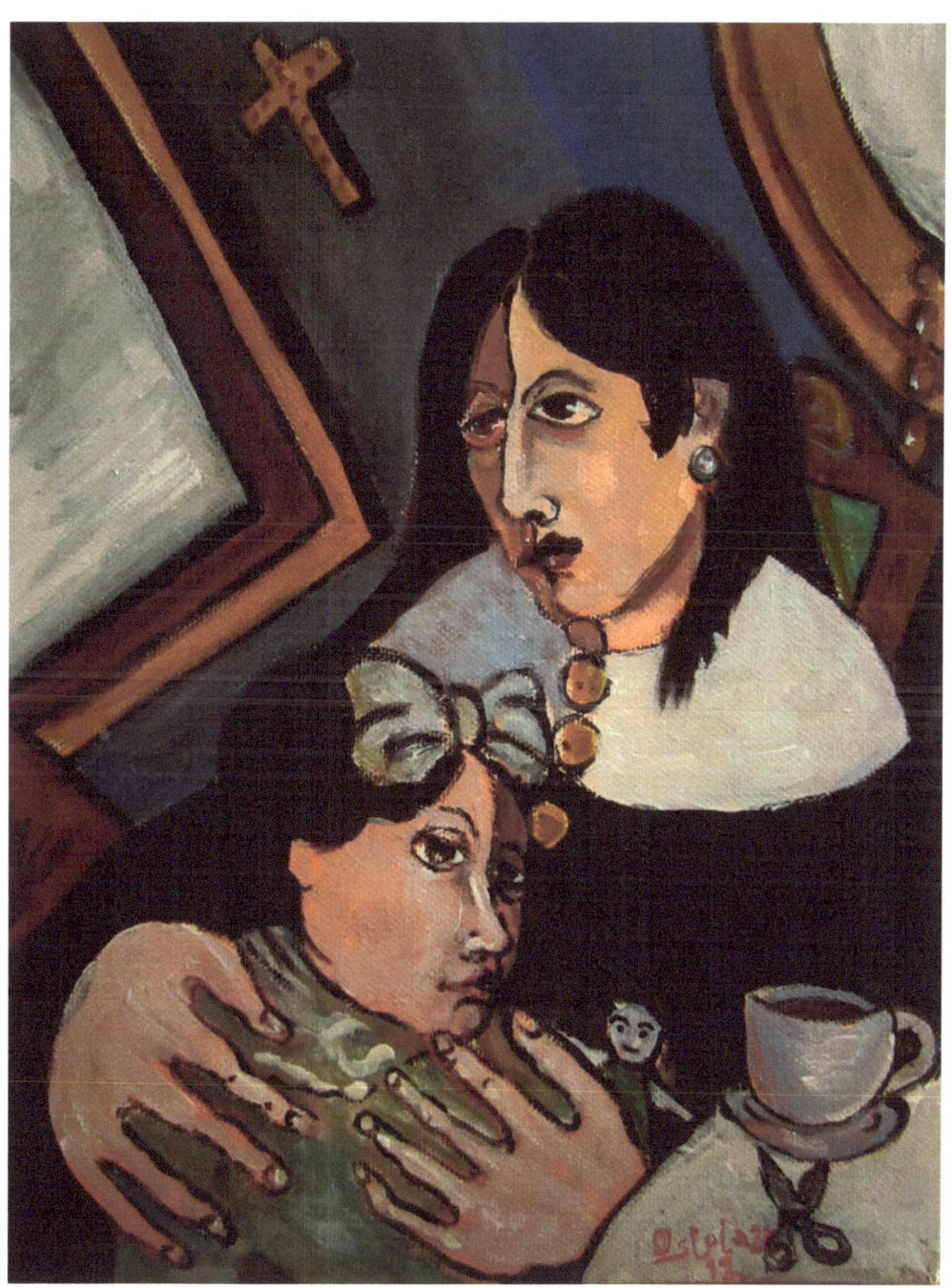

SUSANA
THE NYMPHOMANIAC

Acrylic on canvas / Acrílico sobre lienzo
8 in x 10 in / 20 cm x 25 cm
2012

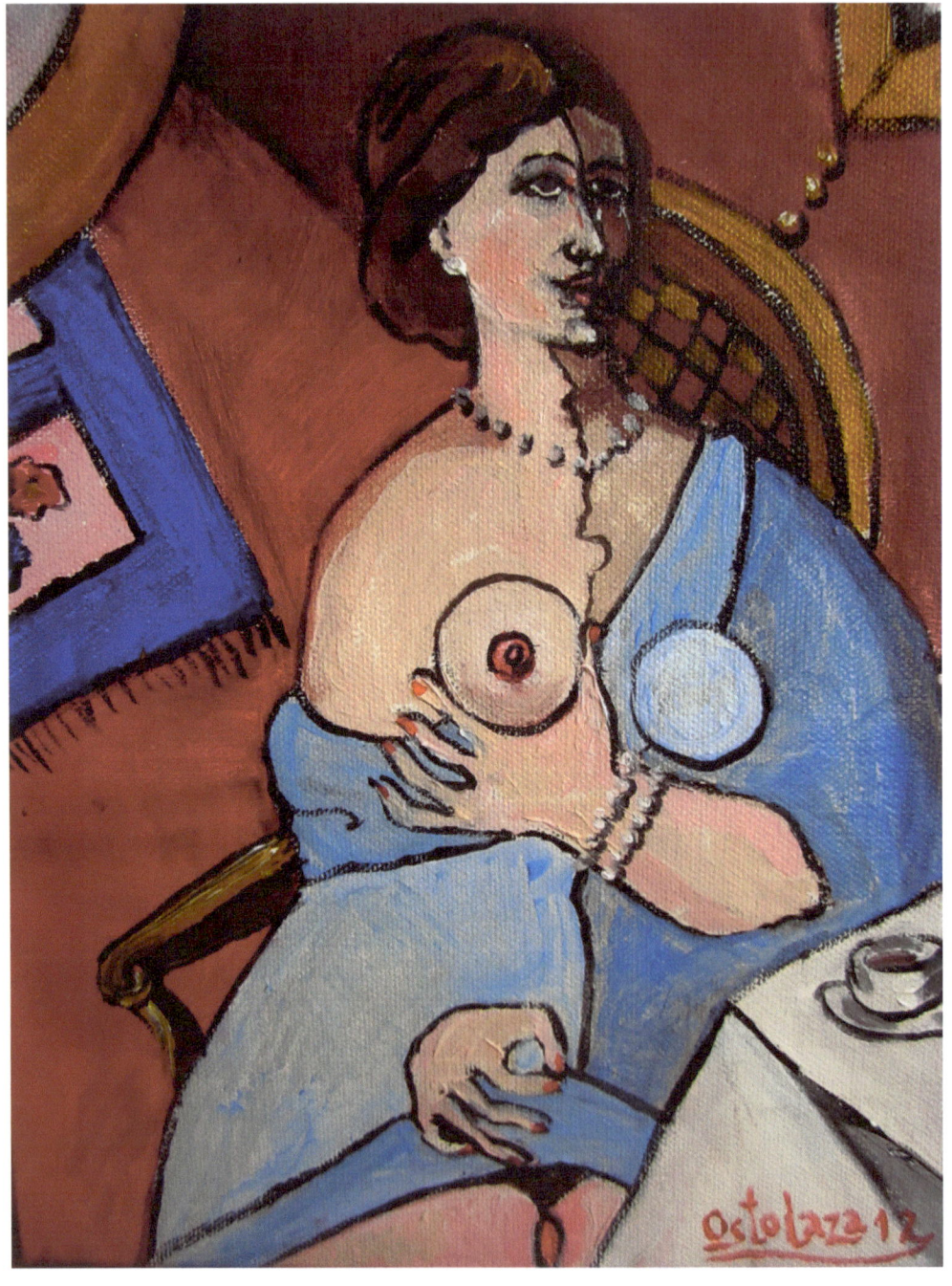

ALICIA
THE GERMAPHOBE

Acrylic on canvas / Acrílico sobre lienzo
5 in x 7 in / 13 cm x 18 cm
2012

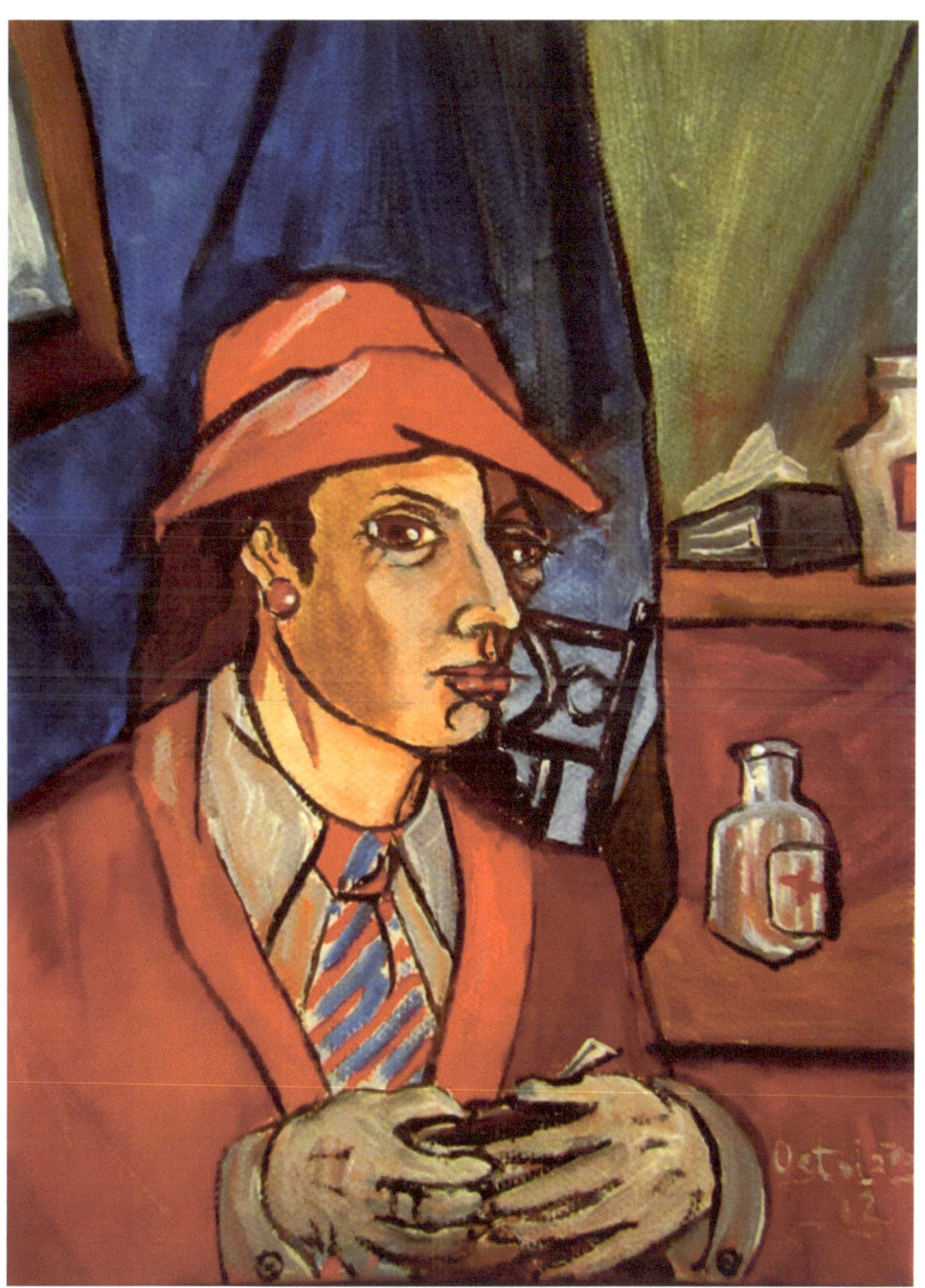

Reneé
The Cartomantic

Acrylic on canvas / Acrílico sobre lienzo
9 in x 12 in / 23 cm x 30 cm
2012

12

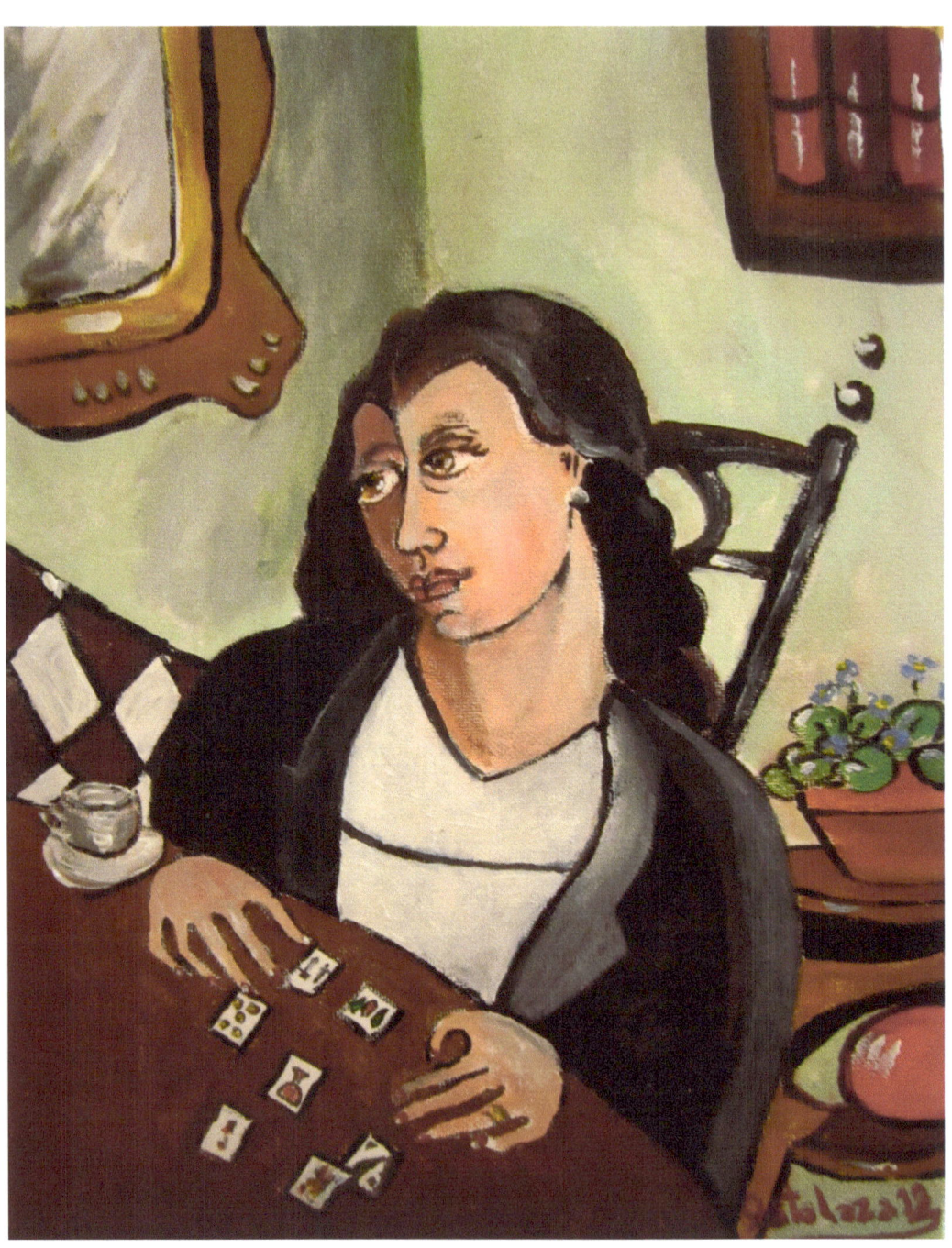

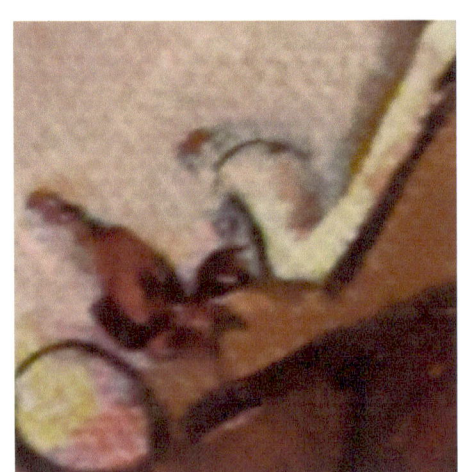

MEAN GIRLS

Semíramis
Queen of Babylon

Acrylic on canvas / Acrílico sobre lienzo
8 in x 10 in / 20 cm x 25 cm
2013

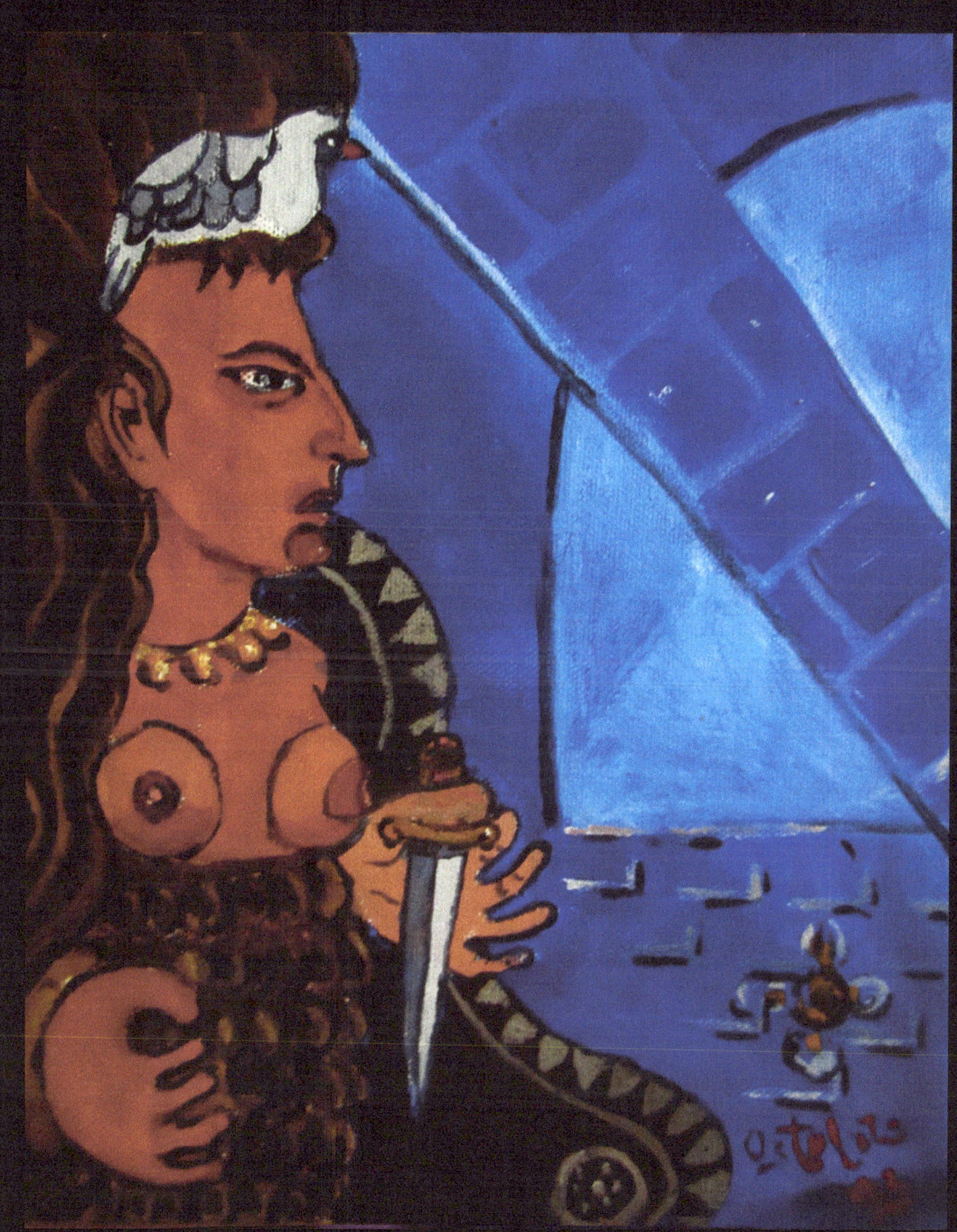

Agripina
Sister of Caligula

Acrylic on canvas / Acrílico sobre lienzo
8 in x 10 in / 20 cm x 25 cm
2013

18

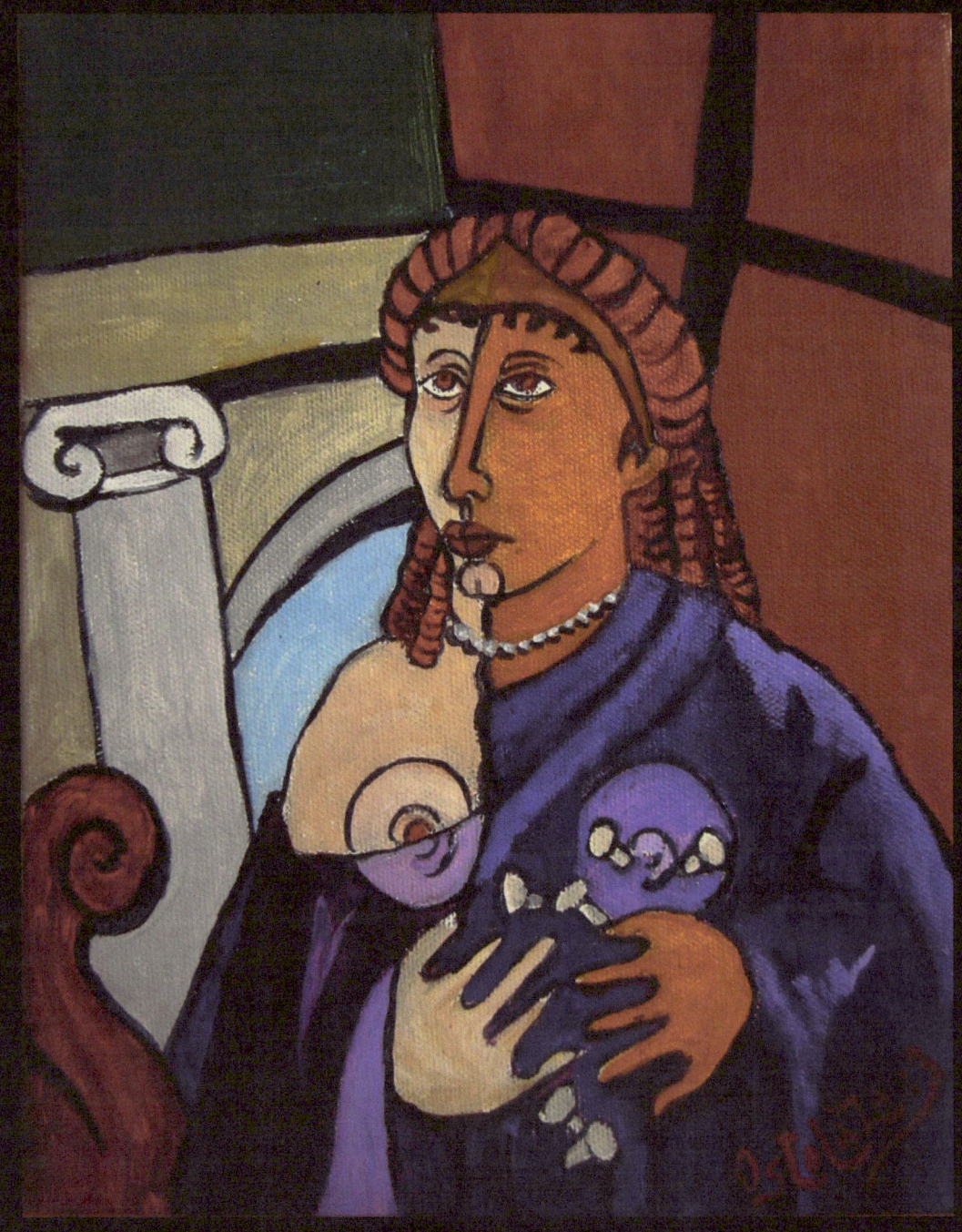

Herodías and Salomé
The Dance of the Seven Veils

Acrylic on canvas / Acrilico sobre lienzo
8 in x 10 in / 20 cm x 25 cm
2013

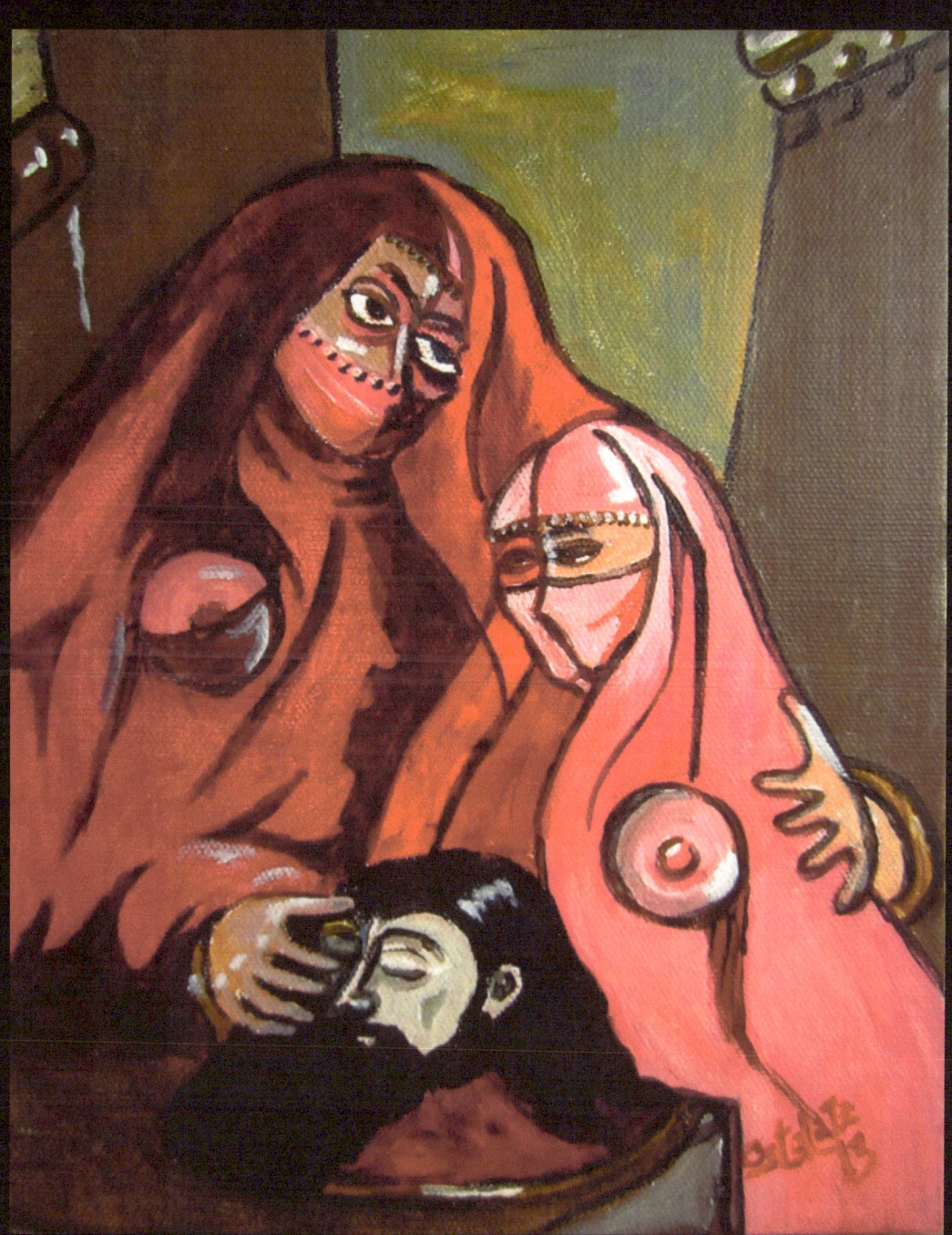

Elizabeth I version 1
The Virgin Queen

Acrylic on canvas / Acrílico sobre lienzo
8 in x 10 in / 20 cm x 25 cm
2013

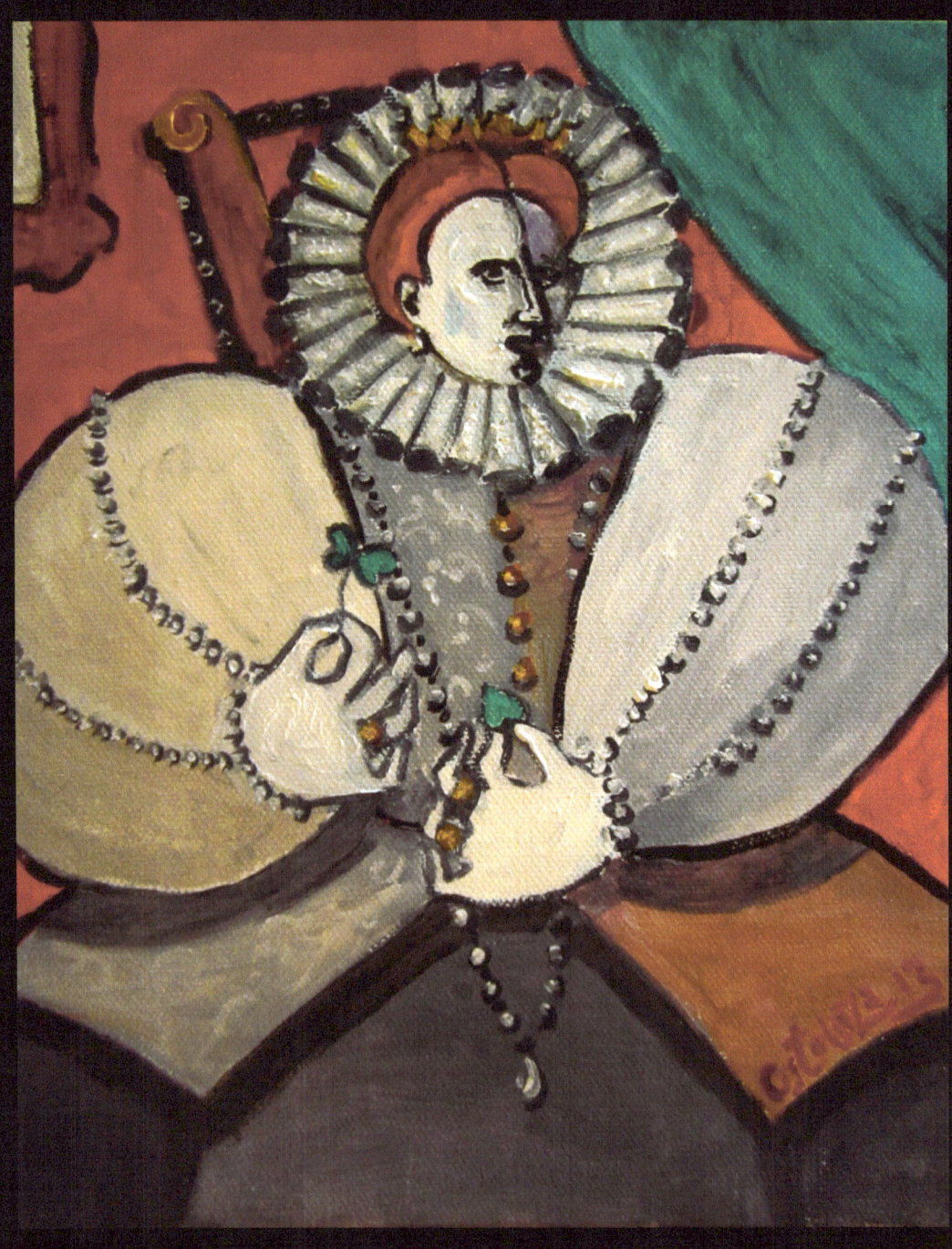

Elizabeth I version 2
The Last of the Tudors

Acrylic on canvas / Acrílico sobre lienzo
8 in x 10 in / 20 cm x 25 cm
2013

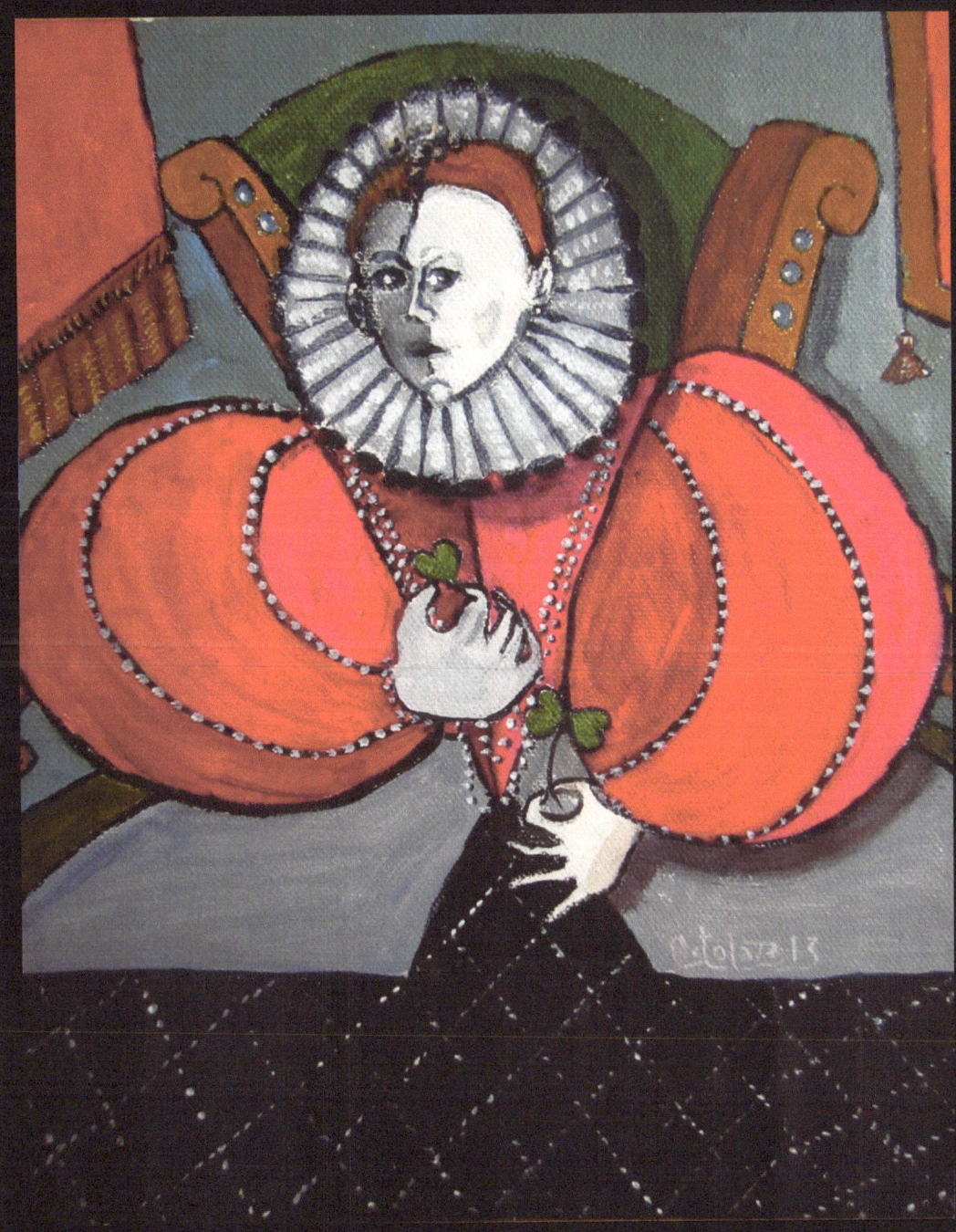

CATHERINE OF MEDICI
THE NIGHT OF SAINT BARTHOLOMEW

Acrylic on canvas / Acrílico sobre lienzo
8 in x 10 in / 20 cm x 25 cm
2013

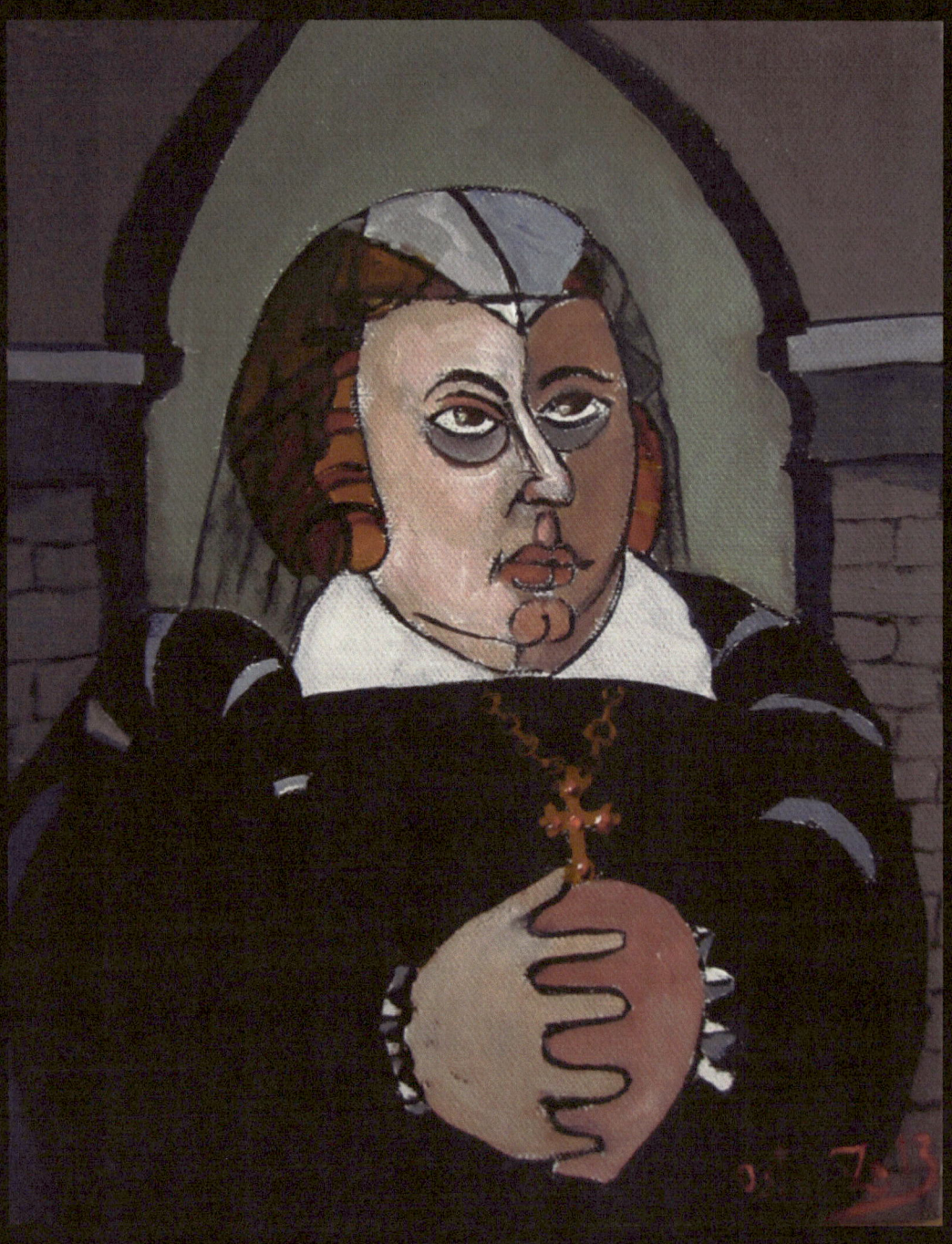

Lucrezia Borgia
The Pope's Daughter

Acrylic on canvas / Acrílico sobre lienzo
8 in x 10 in / 20 cm x 25 cm
2013

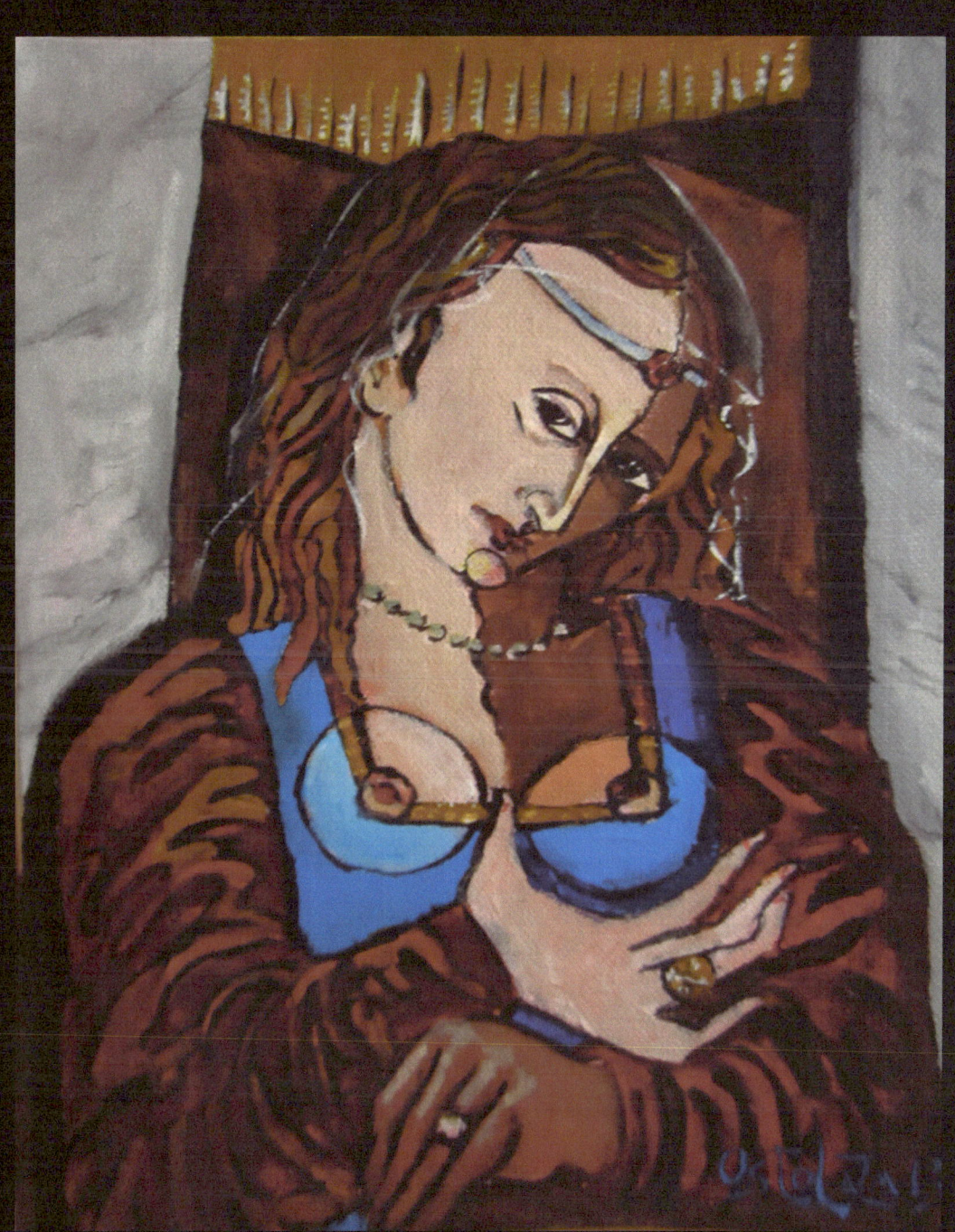

Madame de Montespán
The Mistress of the Sun King

Acrylic on canvas / Acrílico sobre lienzo
8 in x 10 in / 20 cm x 25 cm
2013

24

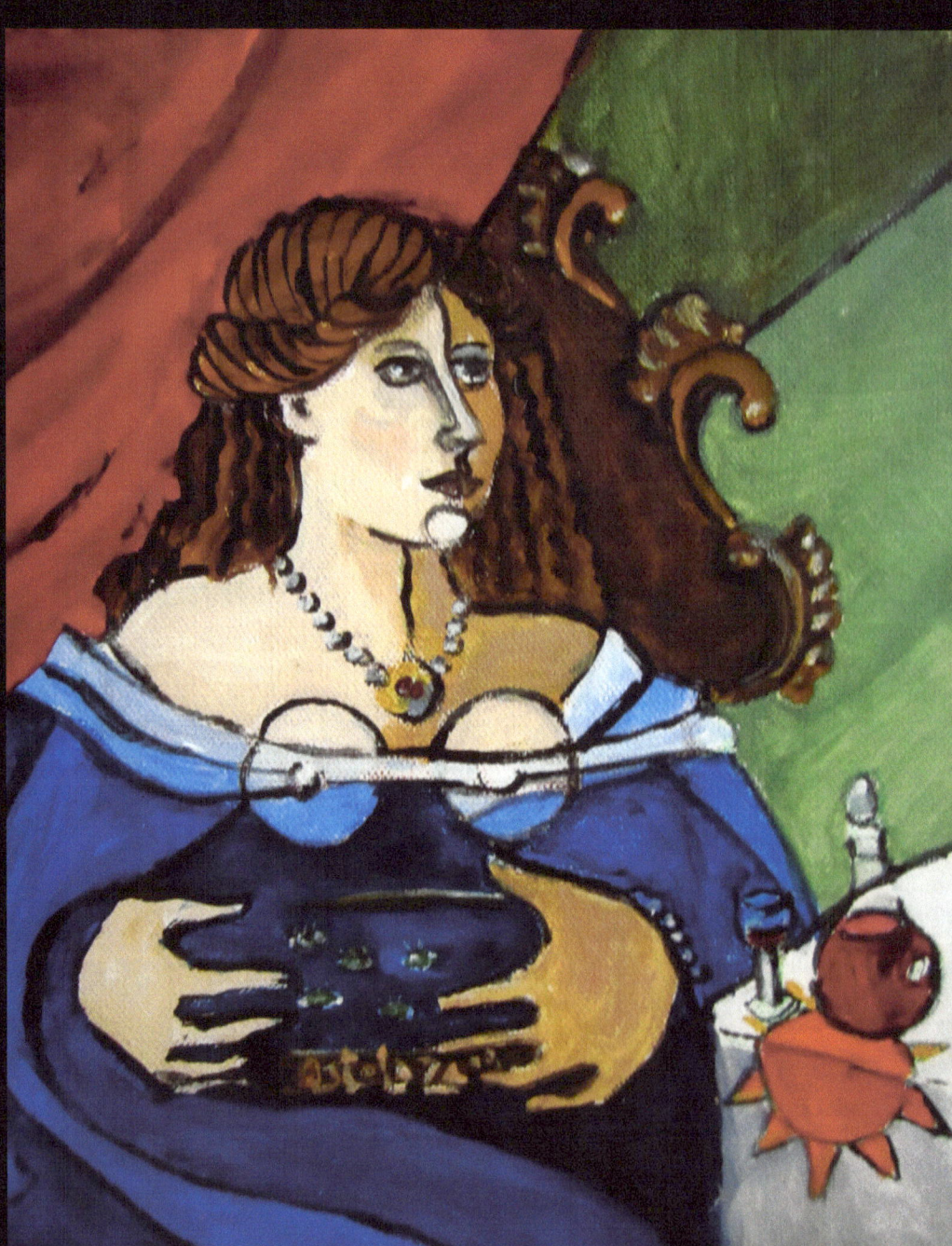

Bonnie Parker

Cigar Smoking Gun Moll

Acrylic on canvas / Acrílico sobre lienzo
8 in x 10 in / 20 cm x 25 cm
2013

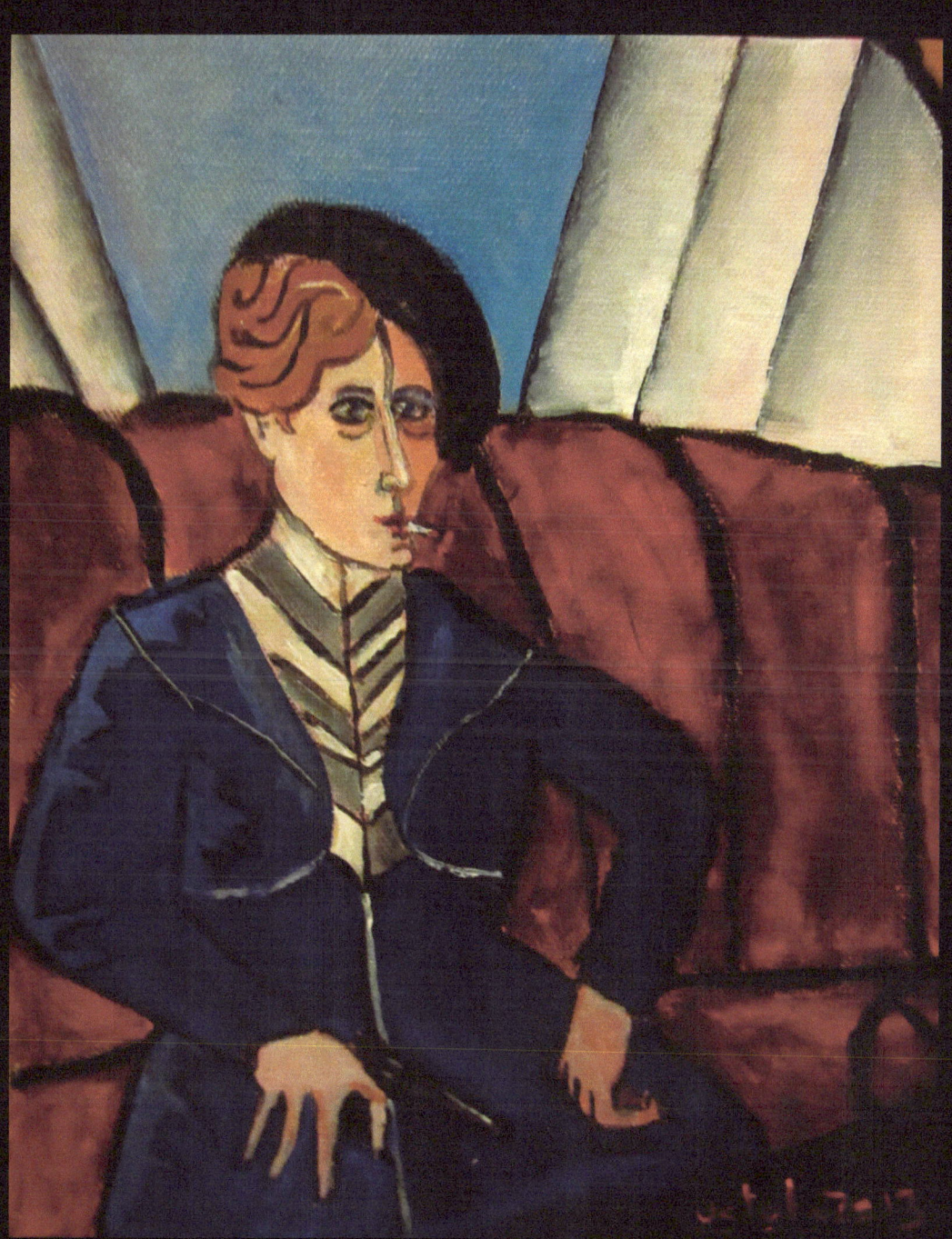

25

Cleopatra
The Siren of the Nile

Acrylic on canvas / Acrílico sobre lienzo
8 in x 10 in / 20 cm x 25 cm
2013

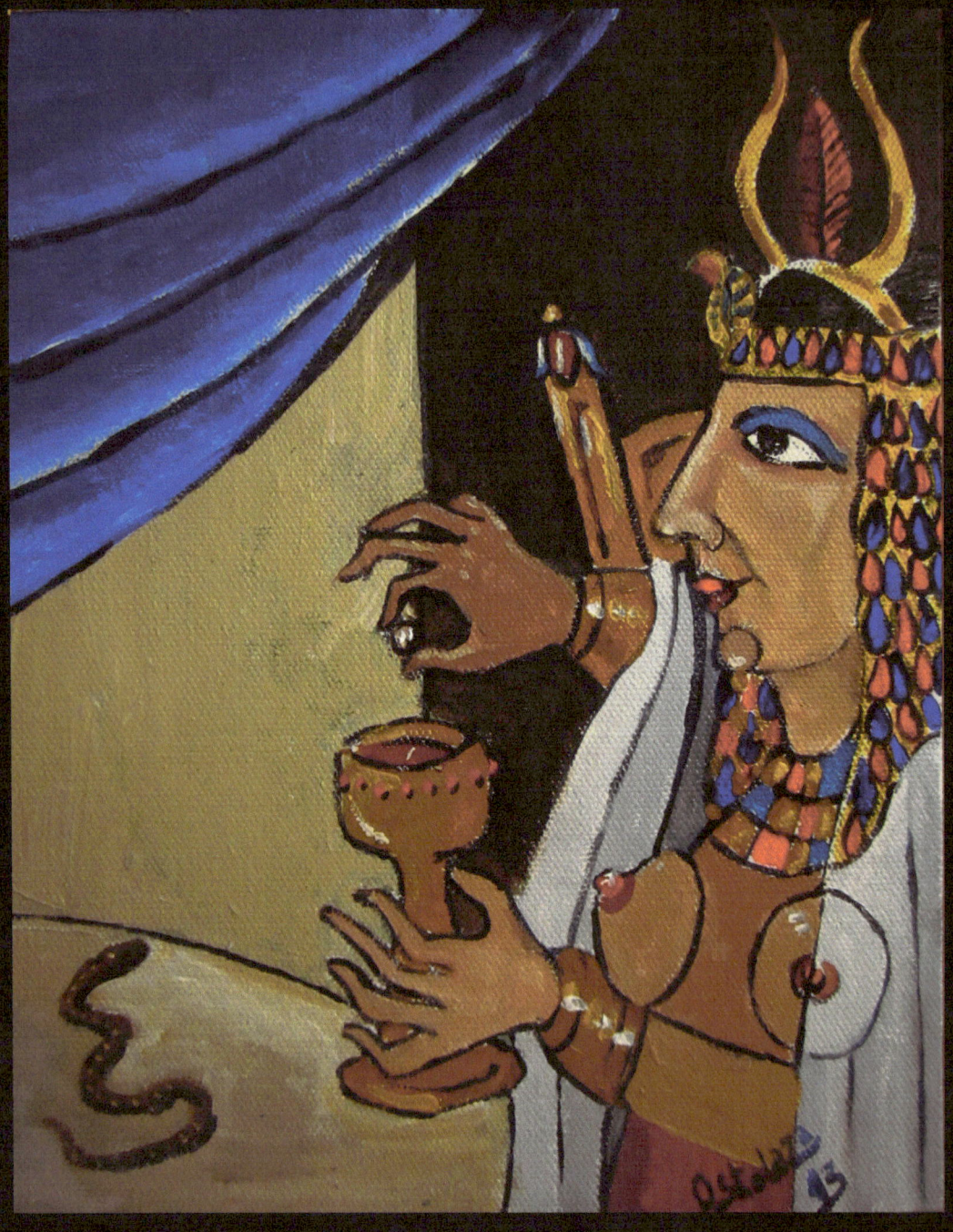

Acrylic on canvas / Acrílico sobre lienzo
8 in x 10 in / 20 cm x 25 cm
2013

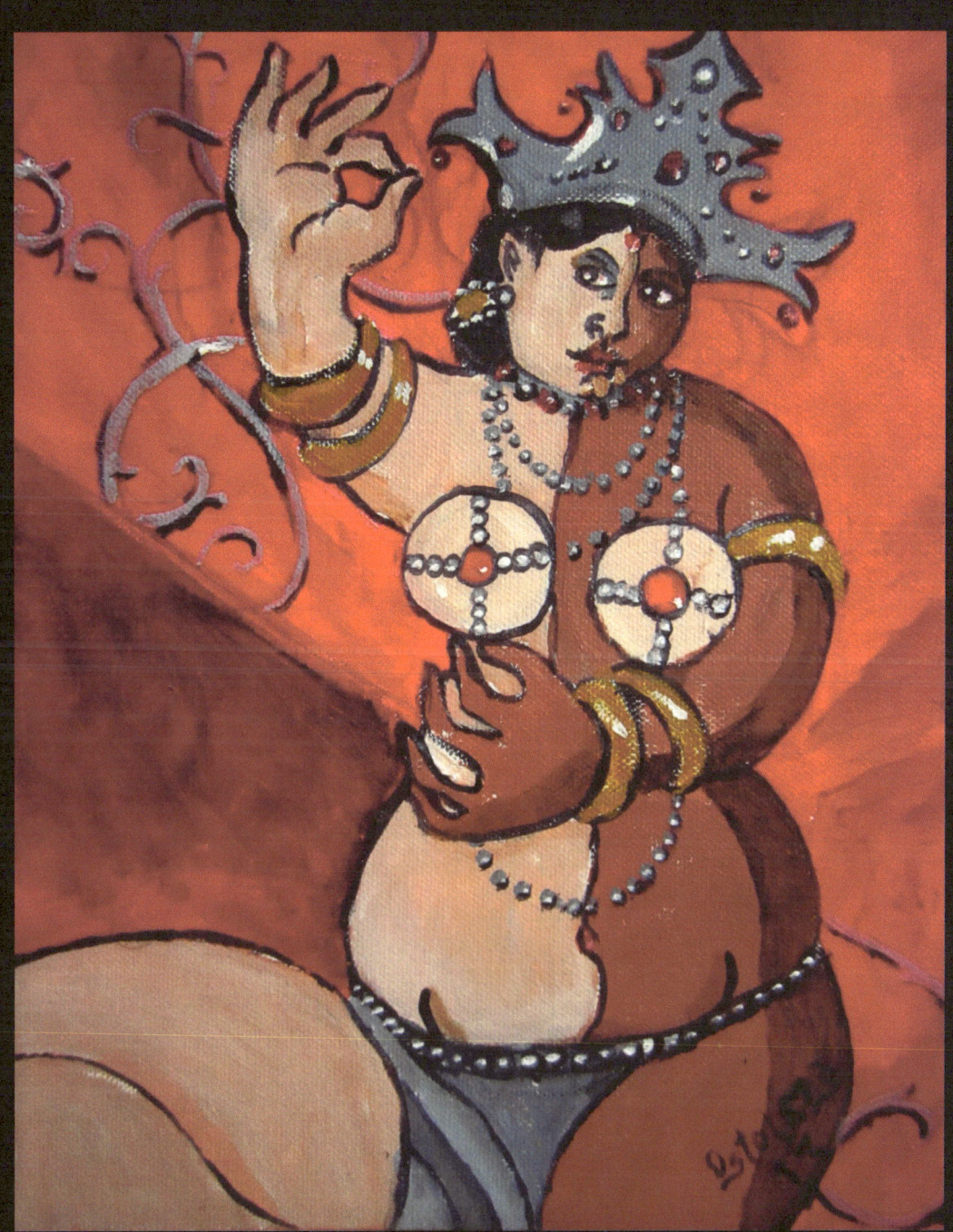

Empress Wu
The Dragon Lady of China

Acrylic on canvas / Acrílico sobre lienzo
8 in x 10 in / 20 cm x 25 cm
2013

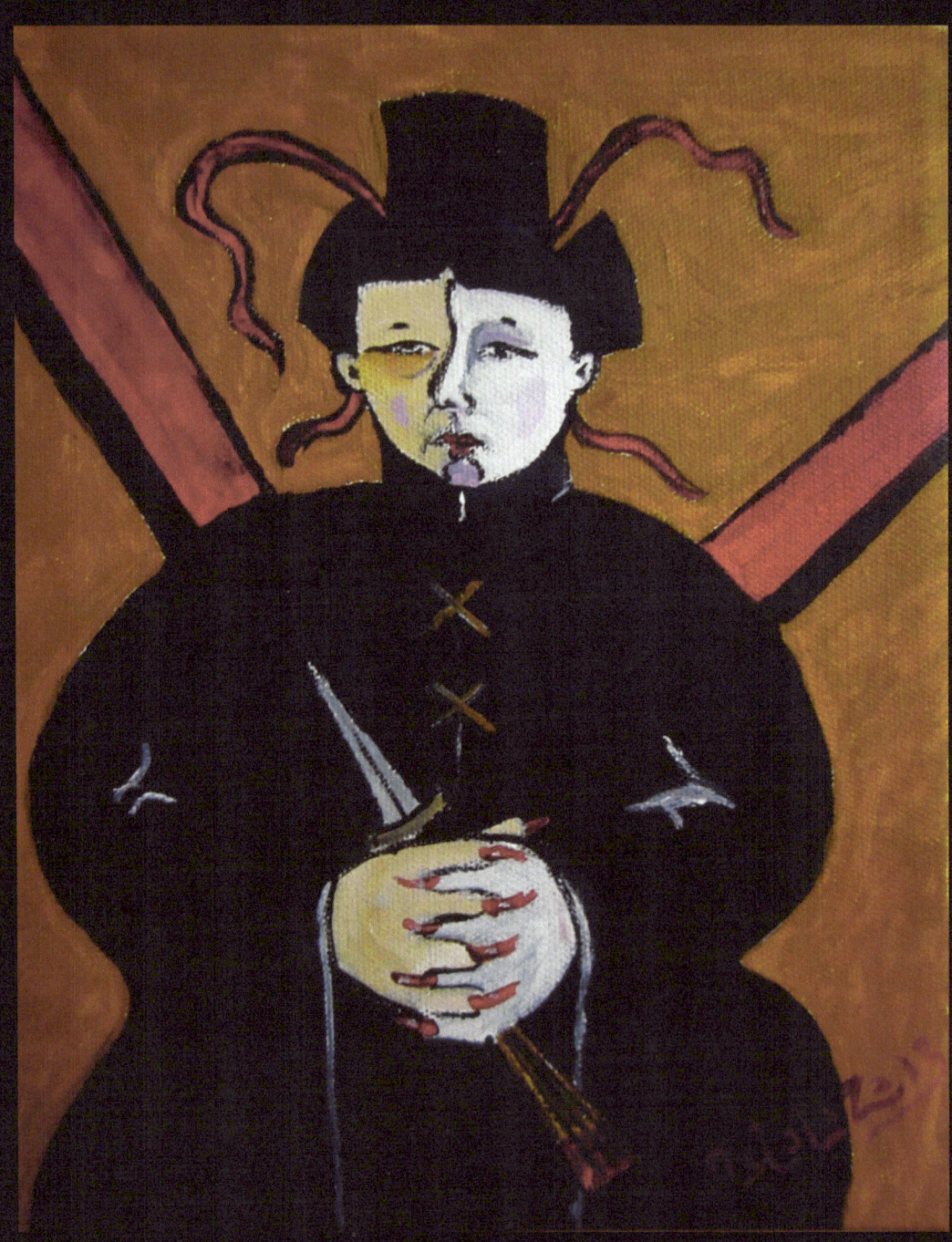

SOME WORDS ON...

Salome

Ah! thou wouldst not suffer me to kiss thy mouth, Iokanaan. Well! I will kiss it now. I will bite it with my teeth as one bites a ripe fruit. Yes, I will kiss thy mouth, Iokanaan. I said it; did I not say it? I said it. Ah! I will kiss it now. But wherefore dost thou not look at me, Iokanaan? Thine eyes that were so terrible, so full of rage and scorn, are shut now. Wherefore are they shut? Open thine eyes! Lift up thine eyelids, Iokanaan! Wherefore dost thou not look at me? Art thou afraid of me, Iokanaan, that thou wilt not look at me?

~ Oscar Wilde from Salome,

Elisabeth I

"I find that I sent wolves not shepherds to govern Ireland, for they have left me nothing but ashes and carcasses to reign over!"

~ Elizabeth I

Mata Hari

"I am a woman who enjoys herself very much; sometimes I lose, sometimes I win."

~ Mata Hari

Lucrecia Borgia

Take the most hideous, the most repulsive, the most complete moral deformity; place it where it fits best --- in the heart of a woman whose physical beauty and royal grandeur will make the crime stand out all the more strikingly; then add to all that moral deformity the purest feeling a woman can have, that of a mother. Inside our monster put a mother and the monster will interest us and make us weep. And this creature that filled us with fear will inspire pity; that deformed soul will be almost beautiful in our eyes..."

~ Victor Hugo
(from the preface to his play "Lucrezia Borgia")

Bonnie Parker

All four Dallas daily papers seized on the story told by the eyewitness, a farmer, who claimed to have seen Parker throw her head back and laugh at the way Patrolman Murphy's head "bounced like a rubber ball" on the ground as she pumped bullets into his prone body.

~ Jeff Guinn in "Go Down Together: The True, Untold Story of Bonnie and Clyde".

Madame de Montespan

The witch and the Madame de Montespan would call on the devil, and pray to him for the King's love. As a way to express her gratitude for her request, they sacrificed a newborn's life by slitting its throat with a knife. Next, the baby's body would be crushed, and the drained blood and mashed bones would be used in the mixture. Louis's food was tainted in this way for almost thirteen years, until the witch was captured after a police investigation where they uncovered the remains of twenty-five hundred infants in La Voisin's garden. In 1666, Madame de Montespan supposedly went so far as to allow a priest, Etienne Guibourg, to perform a black mass over her nude body in a blood-soaked ceremony, which was also said to have included infant sacrifice

~ from the testimony of La Voisin "Madame de Montespan was an habituée of the Abbé Guibourg's infamous Black Mass."

Empress Wu

"With a heart like a serpent and a nature like that of a wolf," one contemporary summed up, "she favored evil sycophants and destroyed good and loyal officials." A small sampling of the empress's other crimes followed: "She killed her sister, butchered her elder brothers, murdered the ruler, poisoned her mother. She is hated by gods and men alike."

~ Mike Dash from "Past Imperfect" http://blogs.smithson-ianmag.com/history/2012/08/the-demonization-of-empress-wu/#ixzz2QTEauv3K

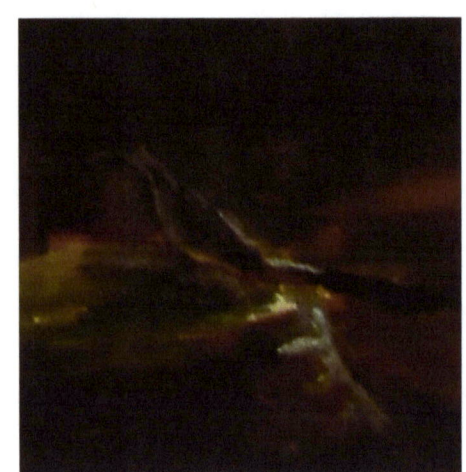

SHAMANS

Shaman I
The Wise Man

Acrylic on canvas / Acrílico sobre lienzo
16 in x 20 in / 41 cm x 51 cm
2013

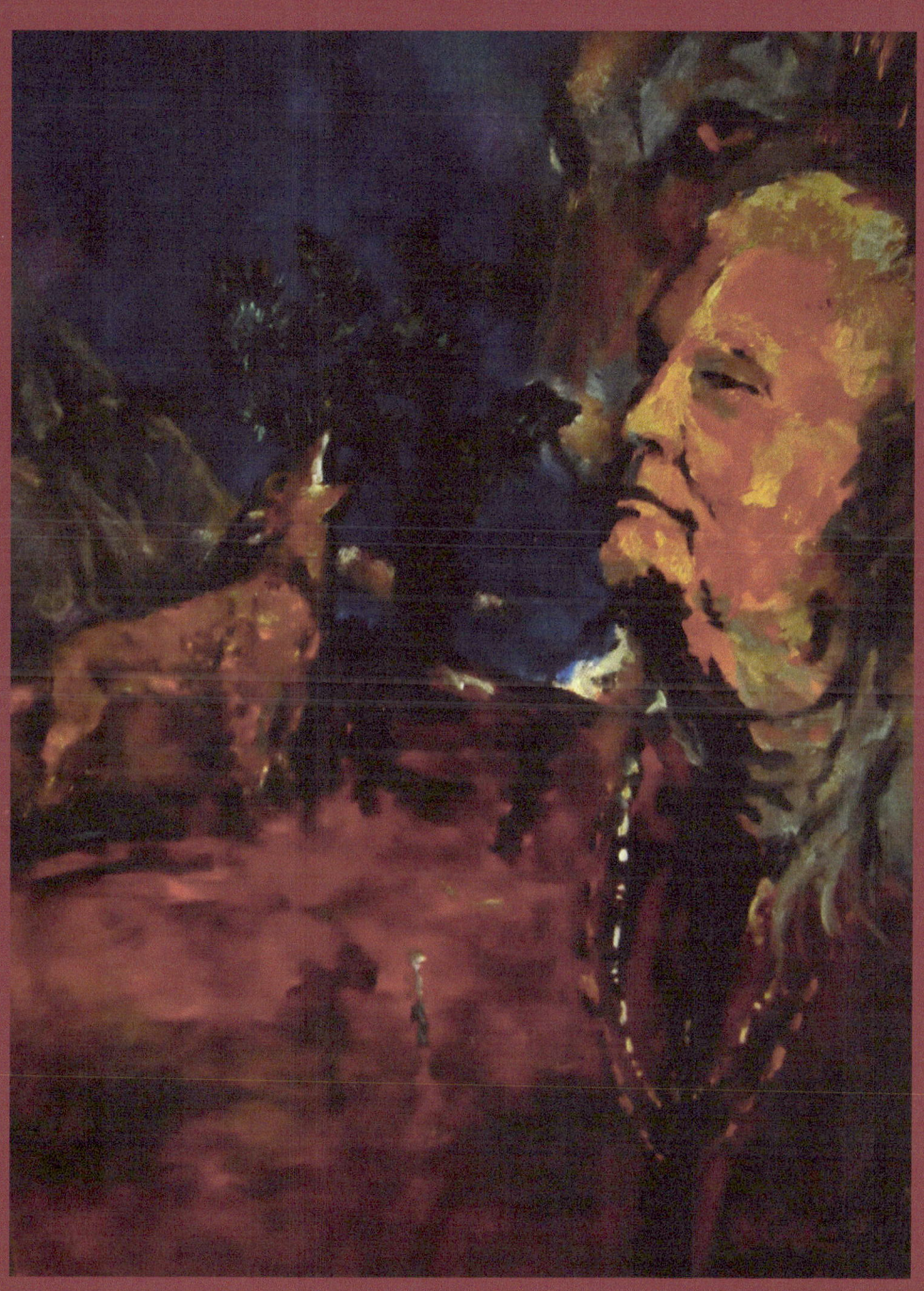

Shaman II
The Provider

Acrylic on canvas / Acrílico sobre lienzo
16 in x 20 in / 41 cm x 51 cm
2013

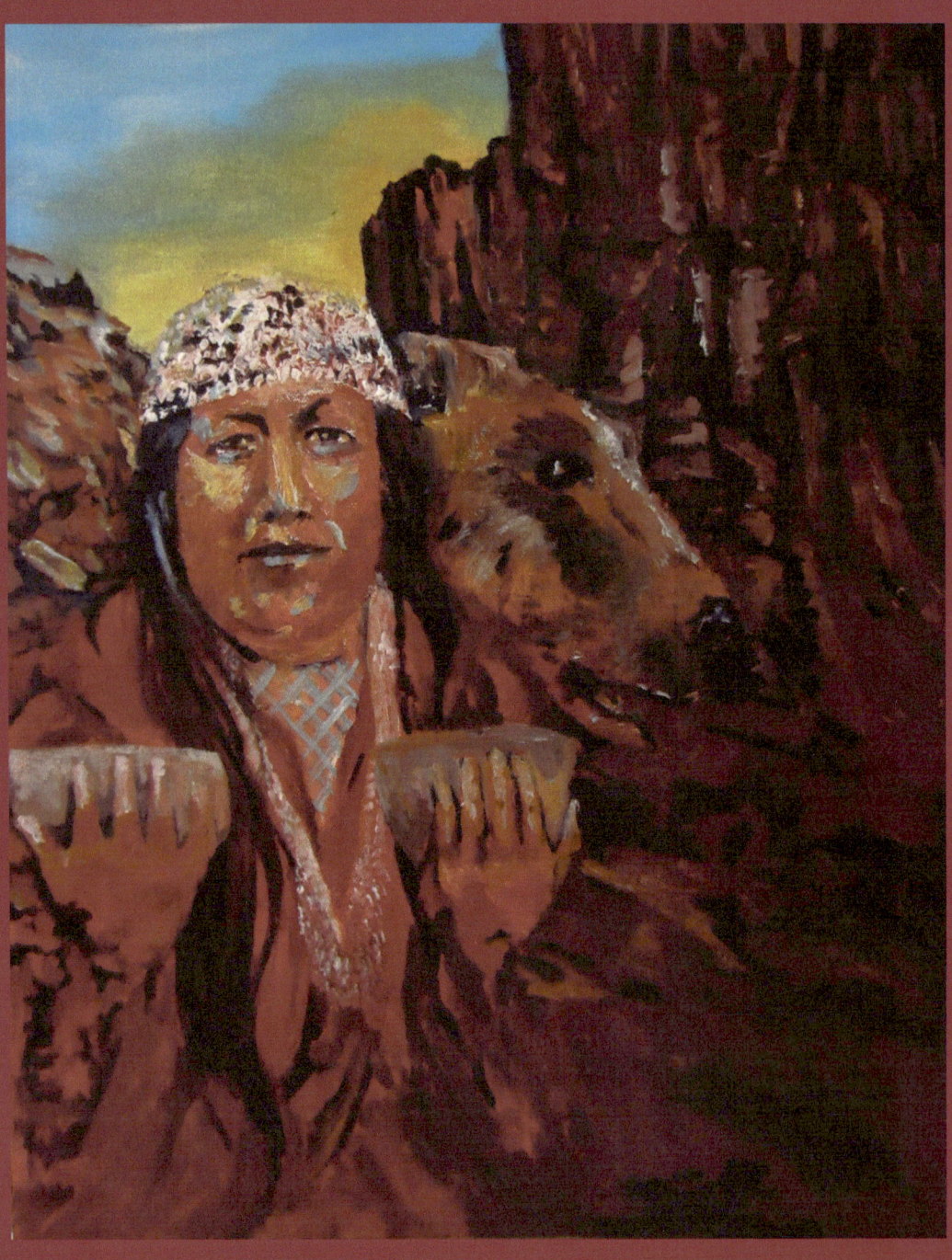

SHAMAN III
THE RAIN DANCER

Acrylic on canvas / Acrílico sobre lienzo
16 in x 20 in / 41 cm x 51 cm
2013

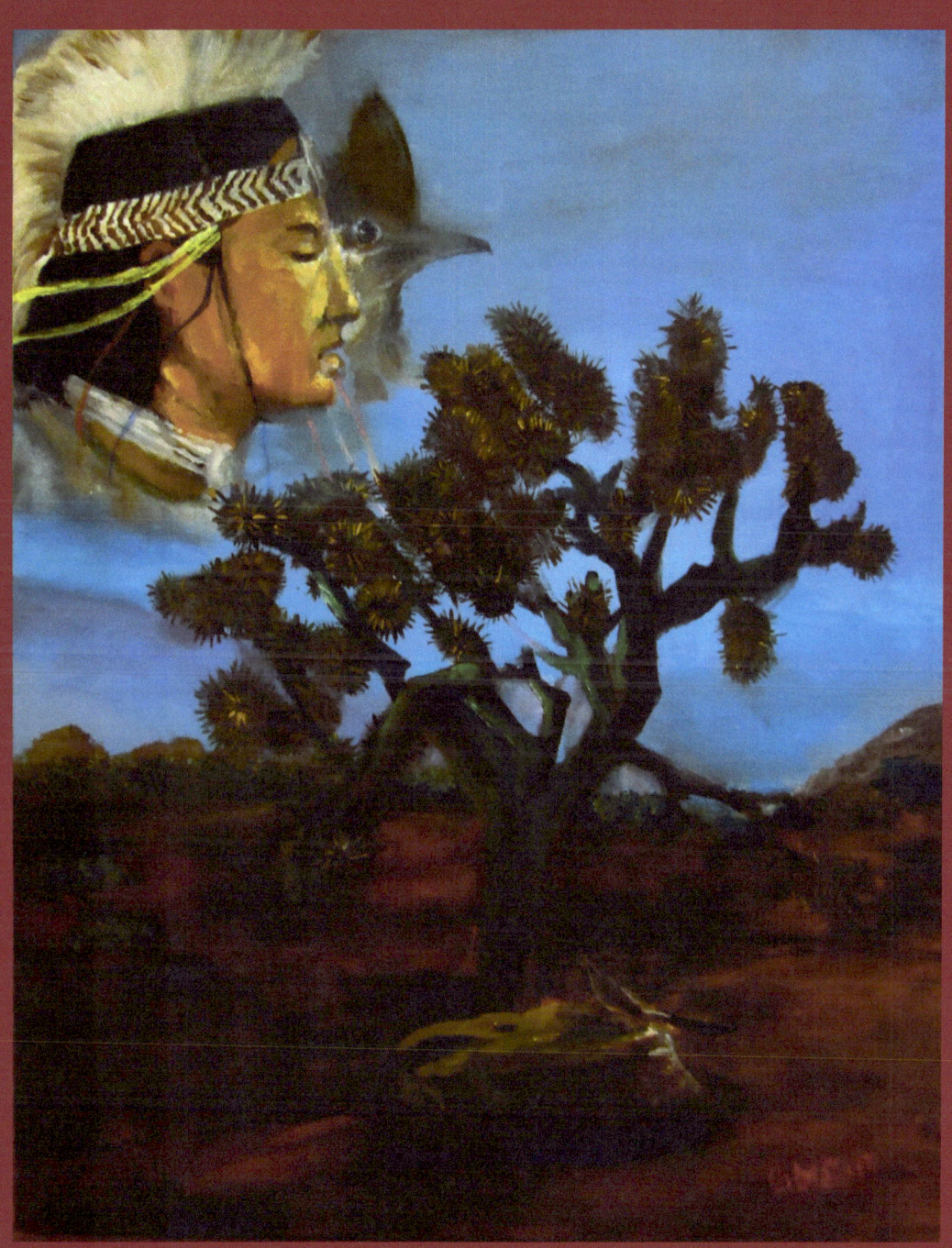

Shaman IV
The Seer

Acrylic on canvas / Acrílico sobre lienzo
16 in x 20 in / 41 cm x 51 cm
2013

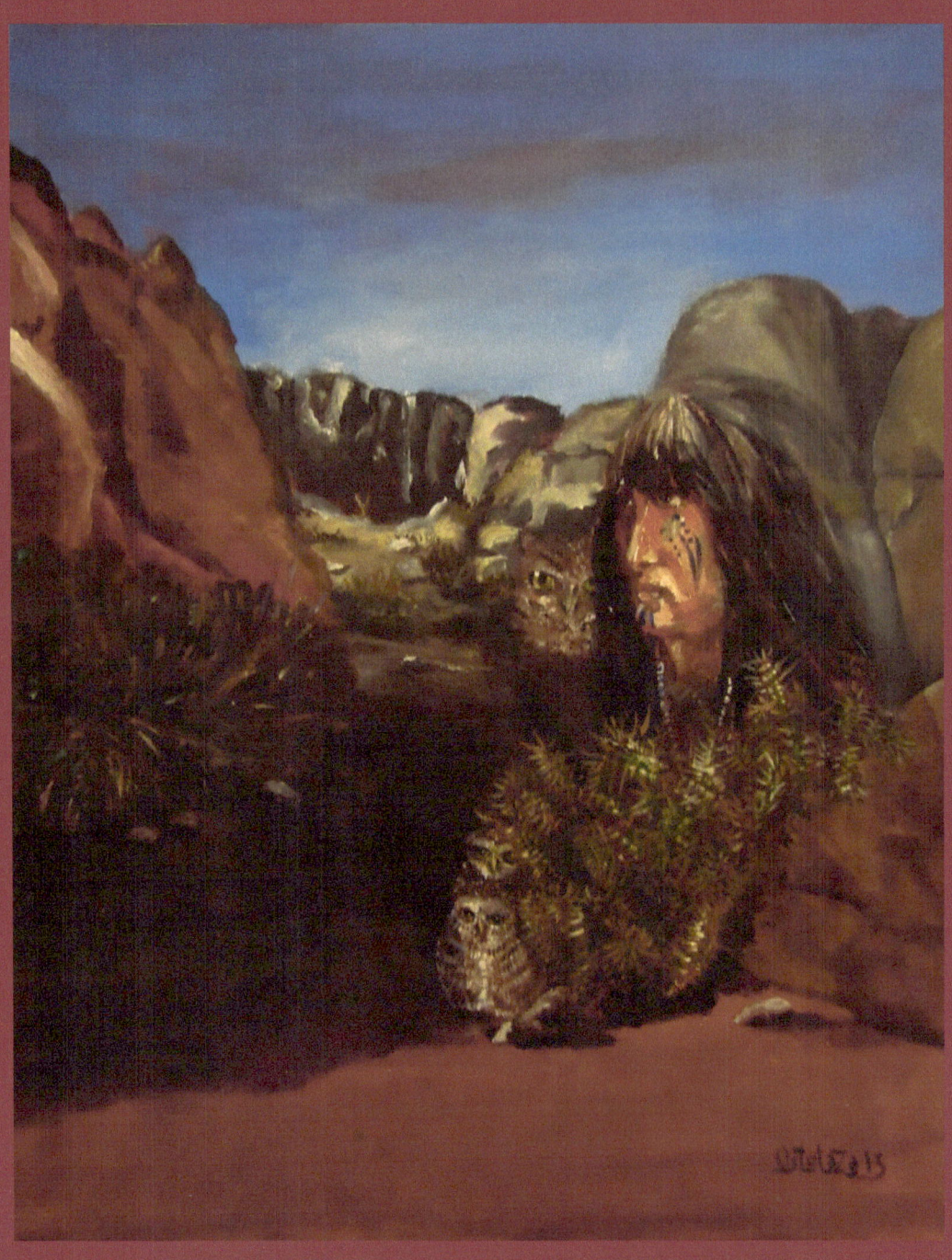

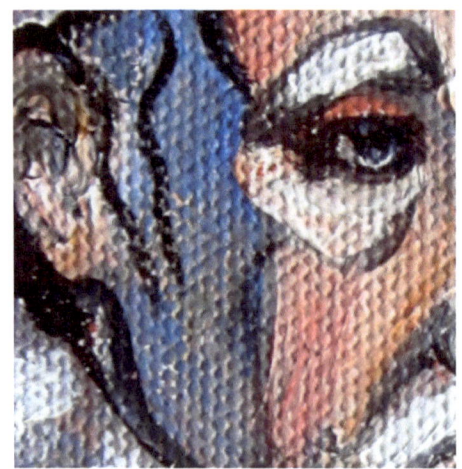

OH MY...!!

AMERICAN DREAM
STARS, STRIPES AND COWBOYS

Acrylic on canvas / Acrílico sobre lienzo
28 in x 39 in / 71 cm x 99 cm
2004

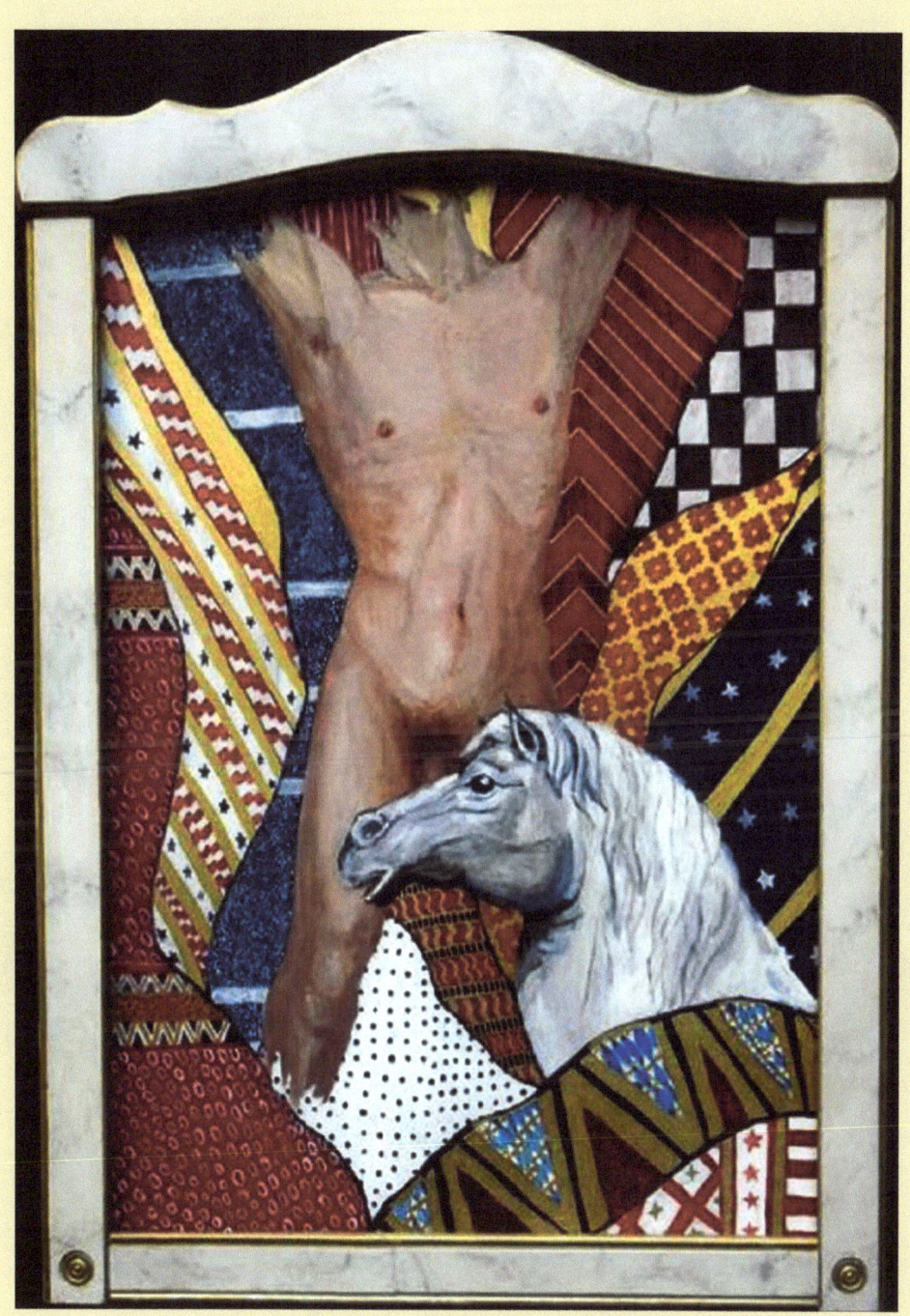

THE THREE GRACES
LIBERTÈ, EGALITÈ, FRATERNITÈ

Acrylic on canvas / Acrílico sobre lienzo
14 in x 11 in / 36 cm x 28 cm
2010

42

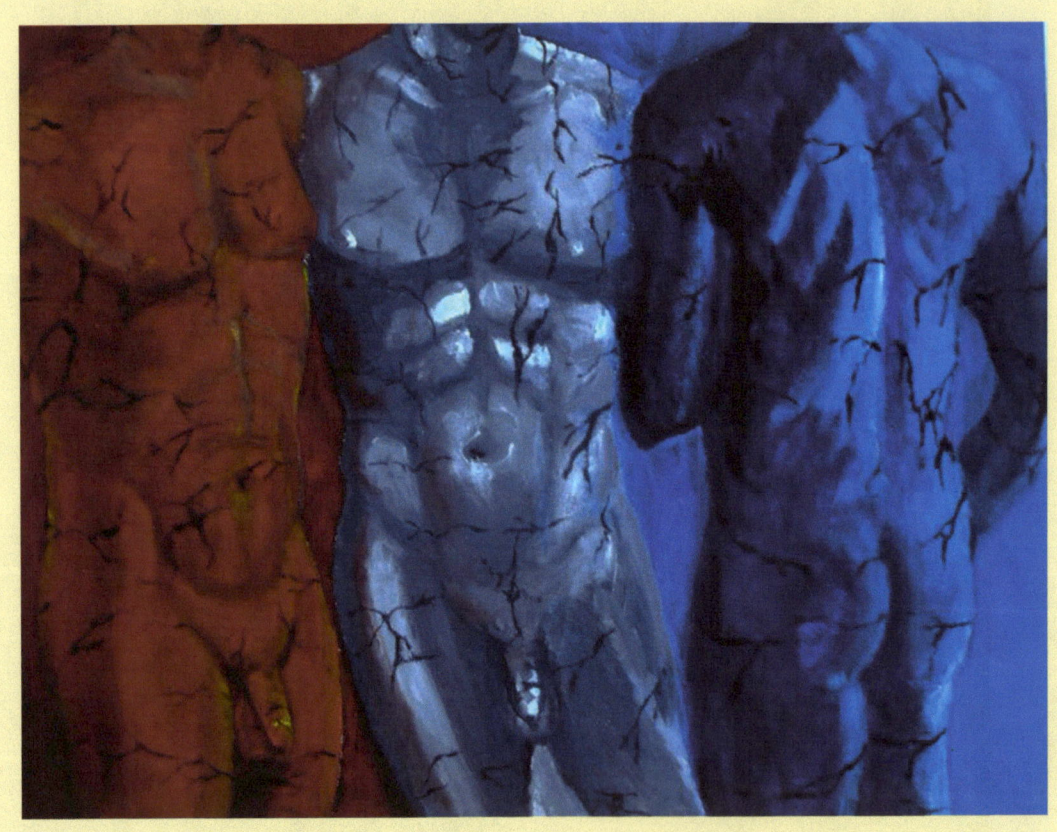

Sebastian of the Border

Frontiers

Acrylic on canvas / Acrílico sobre lienzo
11 in x 14 in / 28 cm x 36 cm
2010

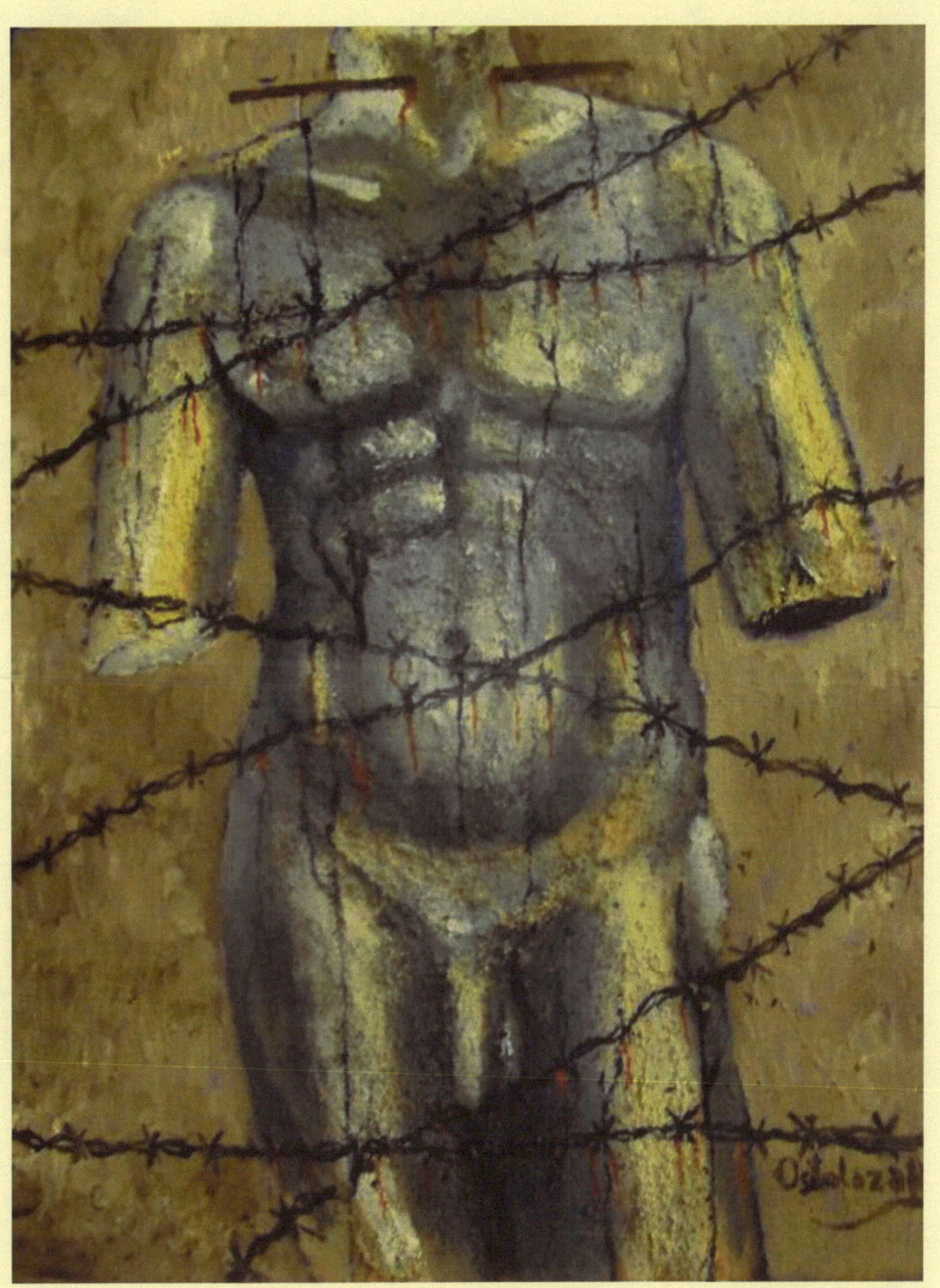

The Birth of Adonis

Rebirth

Acrylic on canvas / Acrílico sobre lienzo
11 in x 14 in / 28 cm x 36 cm
2013

44

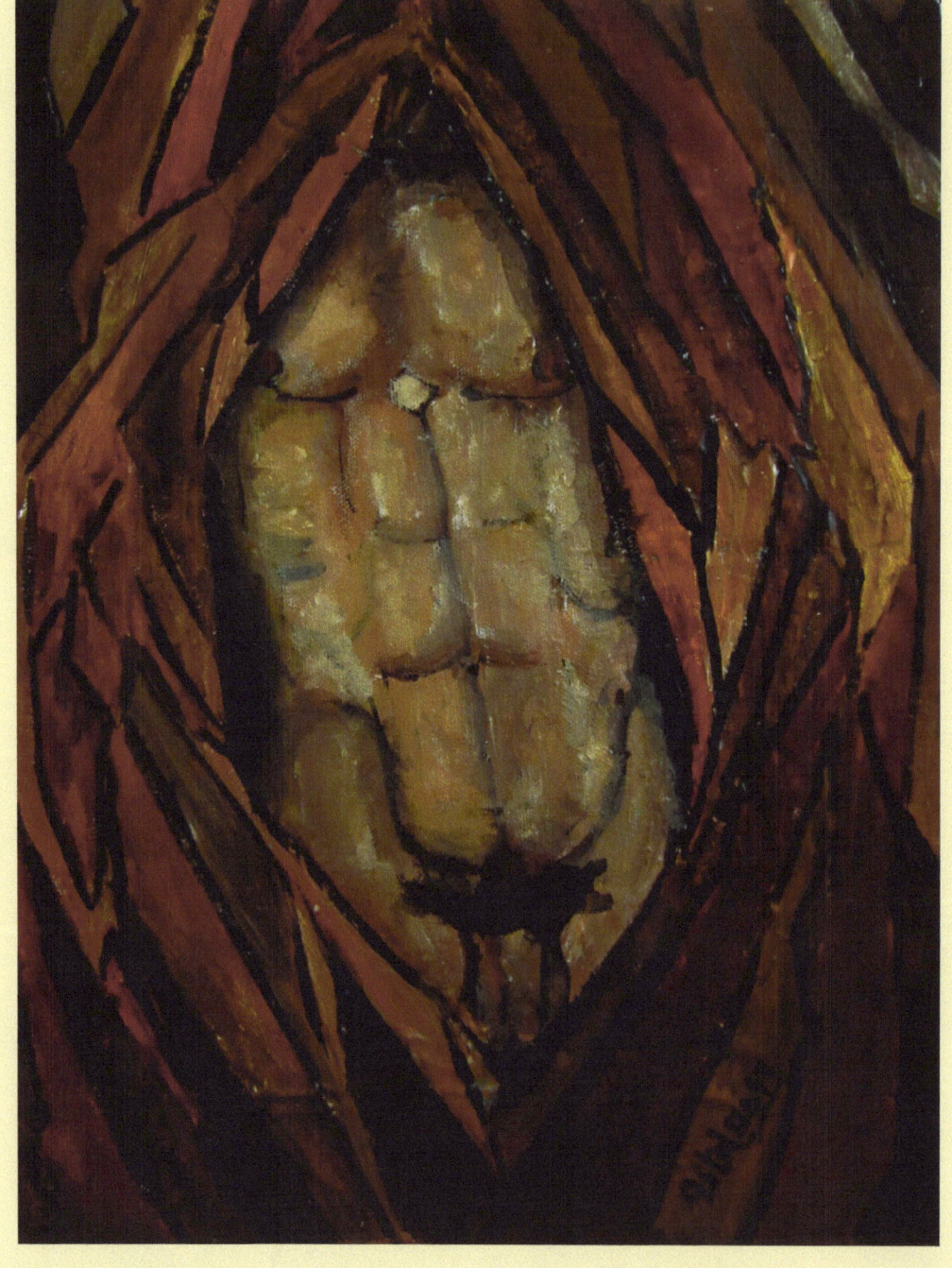

Rebellious Force
Struggle for Liberty

Acrylic on canvas / Acrílico sobre lienzo
11 in x 14 / 28 cm x 36 cm
2012

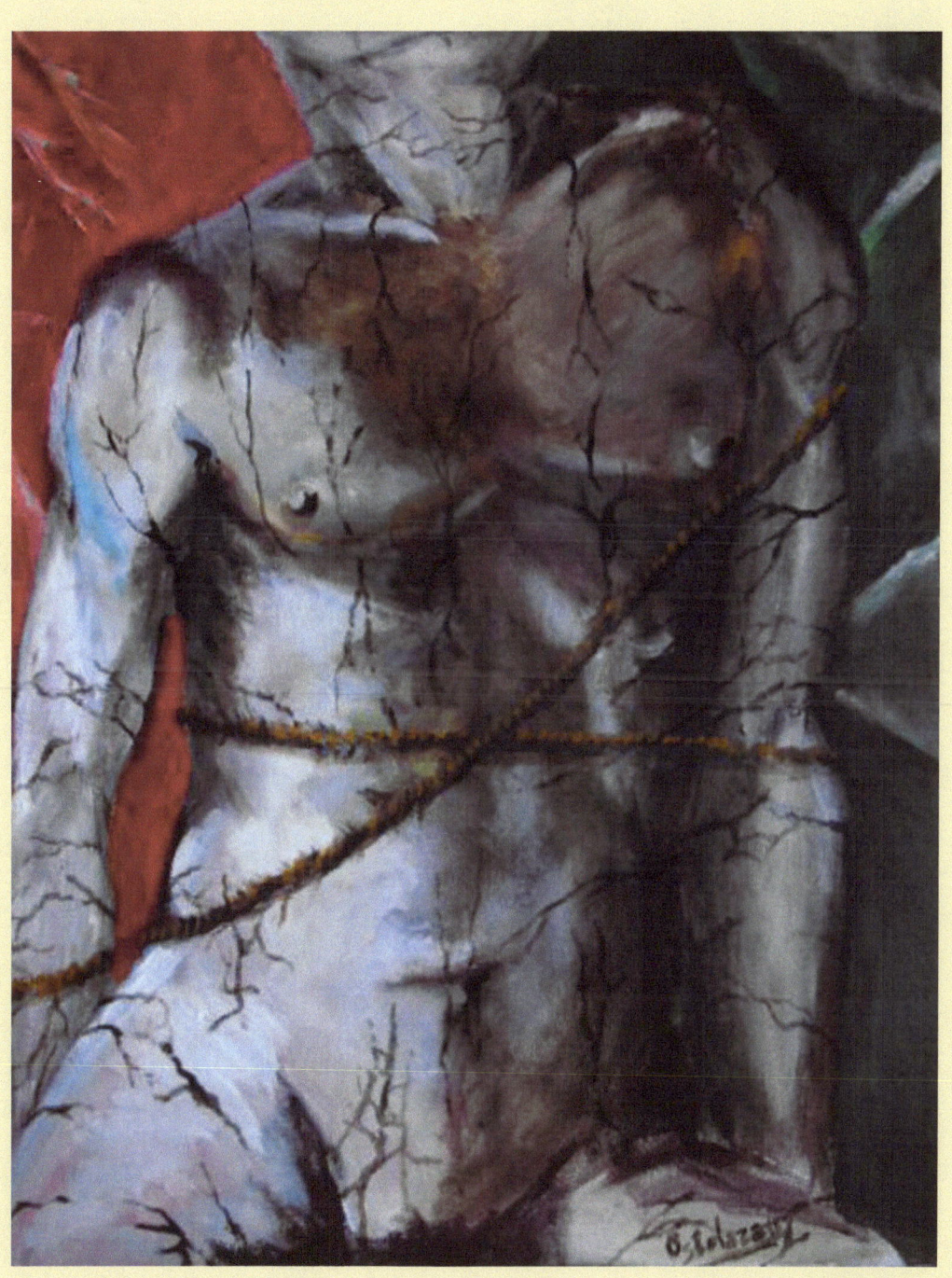

Pacific Resistance
Abuse of Power

Acrylic on canvas / Acrílico sobre lienzo
9 in x 12 in / 23 cm x 30 cm
2013

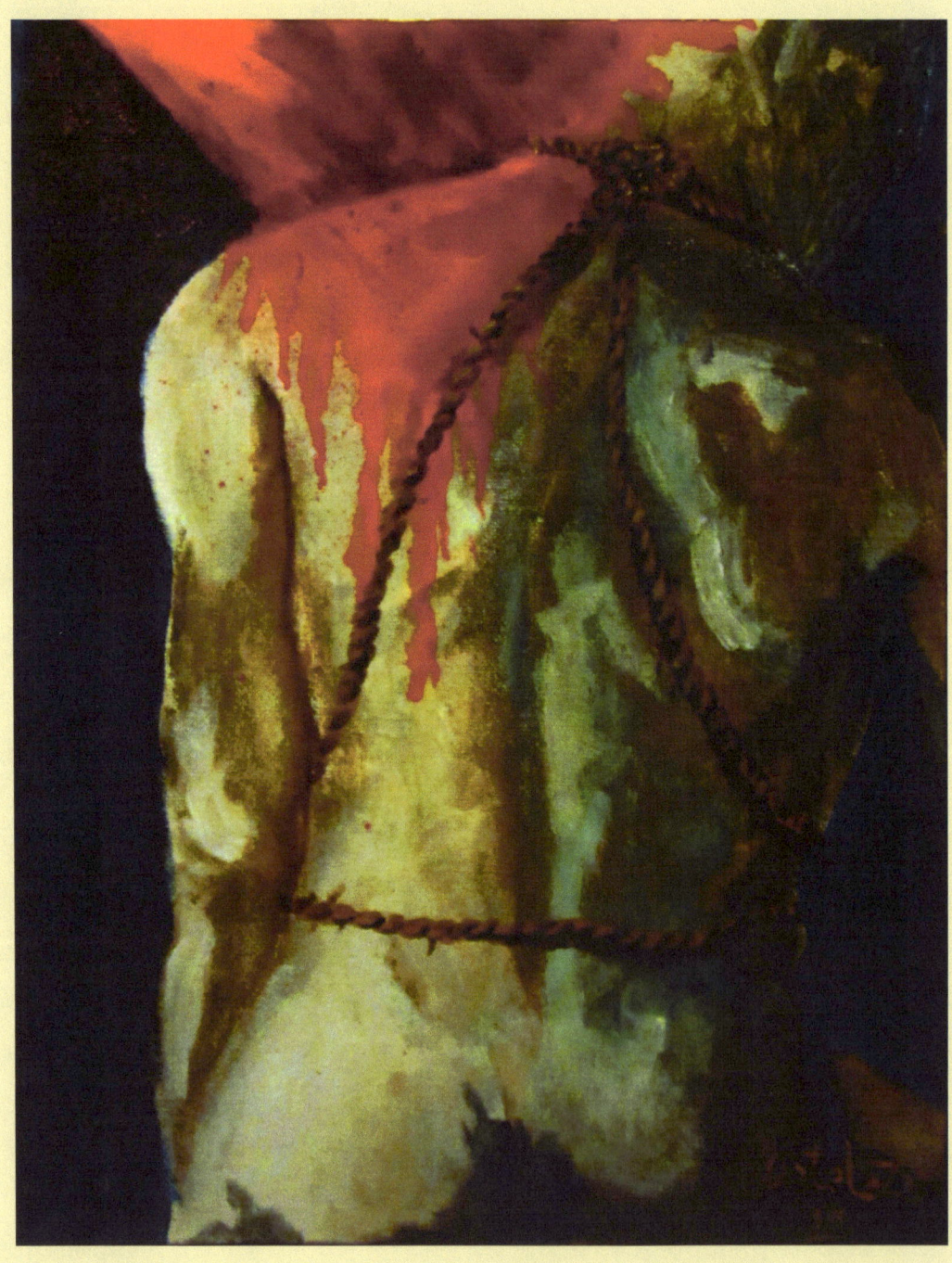

TWILIGHT OF THE GODS
THE END OF THE TRADITIONS

Acrylic on canvas / Acrílico sobre lienzo
11 in x 14 in / 28 cm x 36 cm
2011

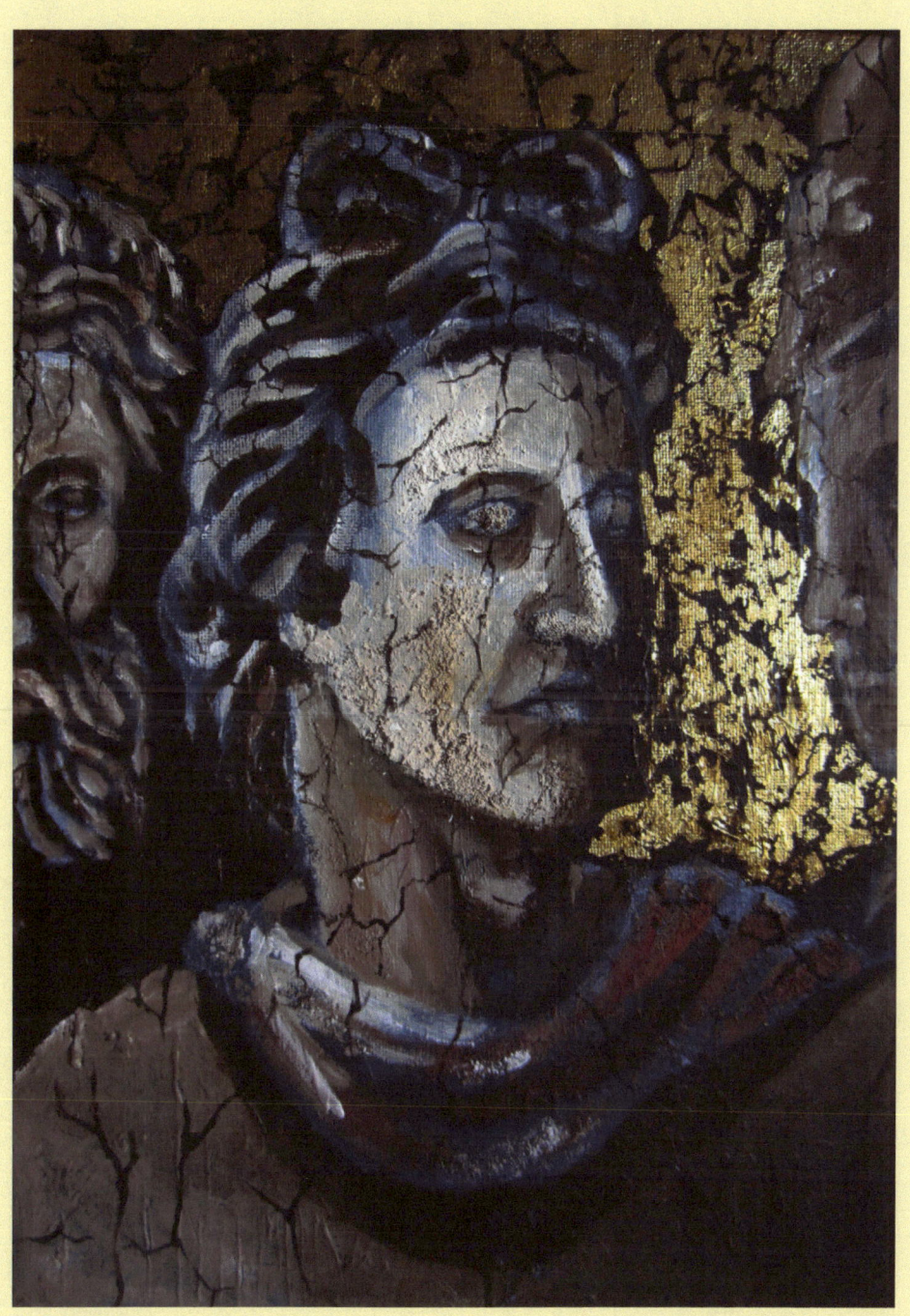

DON QUIXOTE
THE DREAMER

Acrylic on canvas / Acrílico sobre lienzo
5 in x 7 in / 13 cm x 18 cm
2012

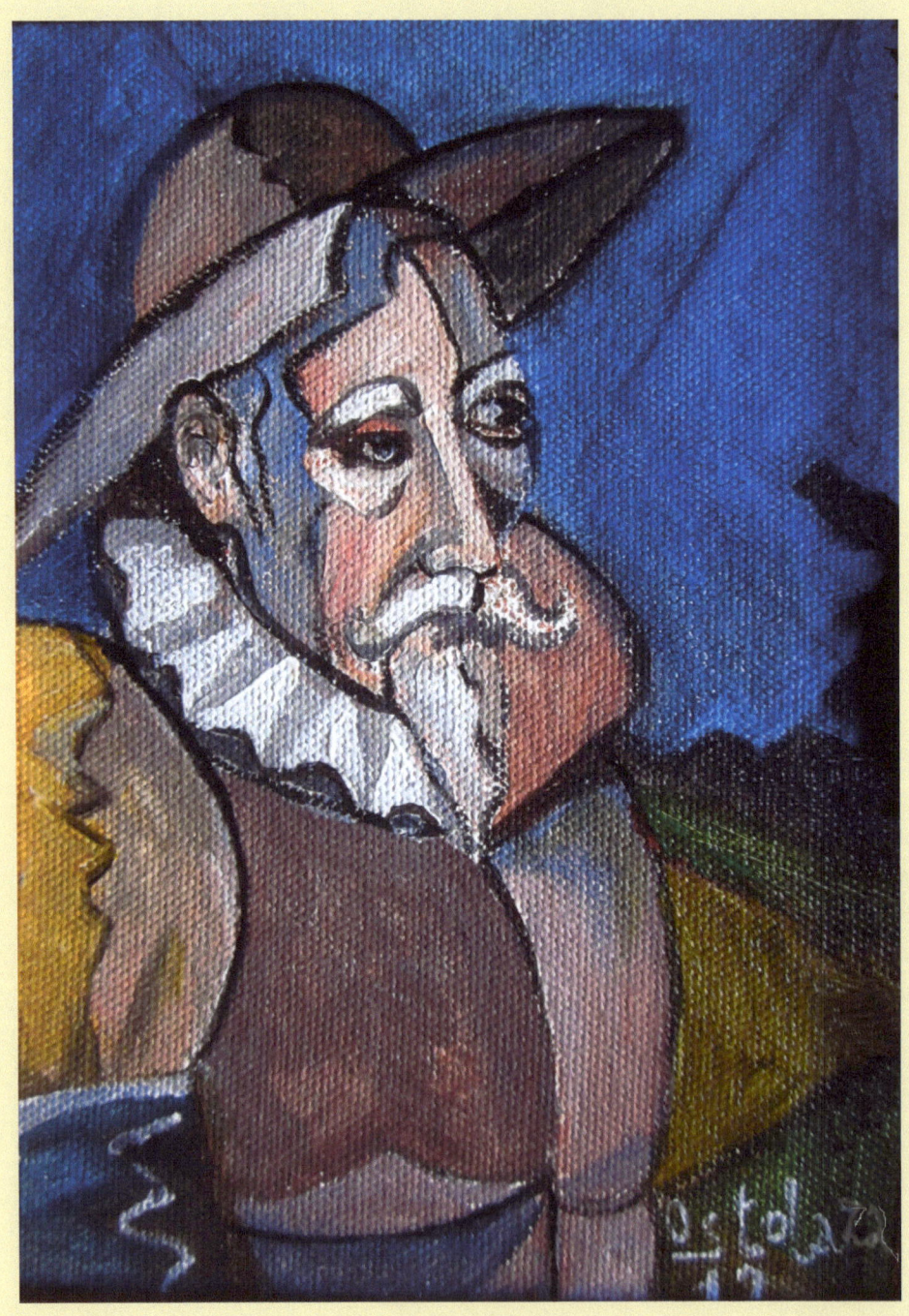

Two Moods
Pierrot and Harlequin

Acrylic on canvas / Acrílico sobre lienzo
5 in x 7 in / 13 cm x 18 cm
2013

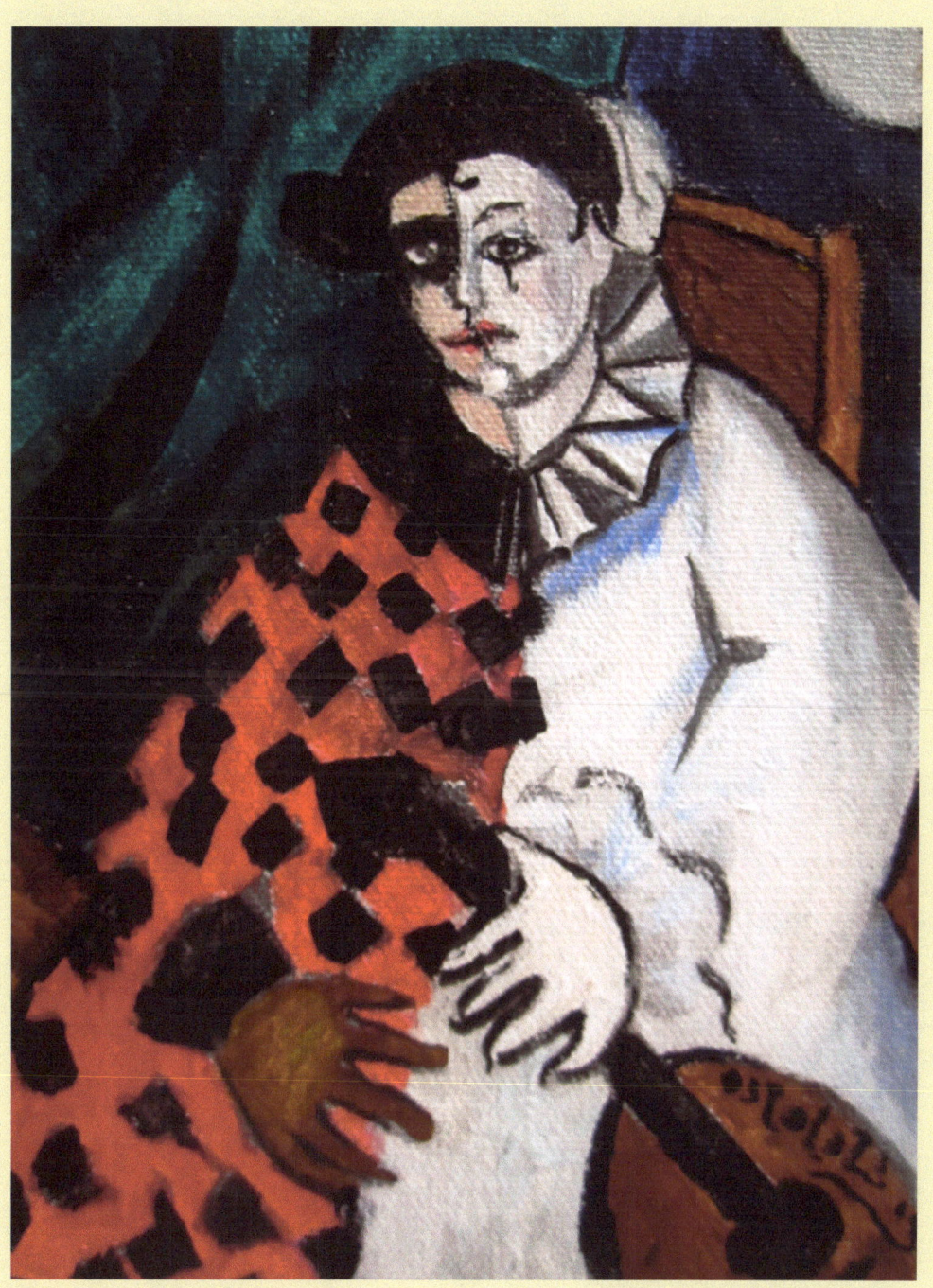

JUGGLER
LET ME ENTERTAIN YOU

Acrylic on canvas / Acrílico sobre lienzo
6 in x 8 in / 15 cm x 20 cm
2013

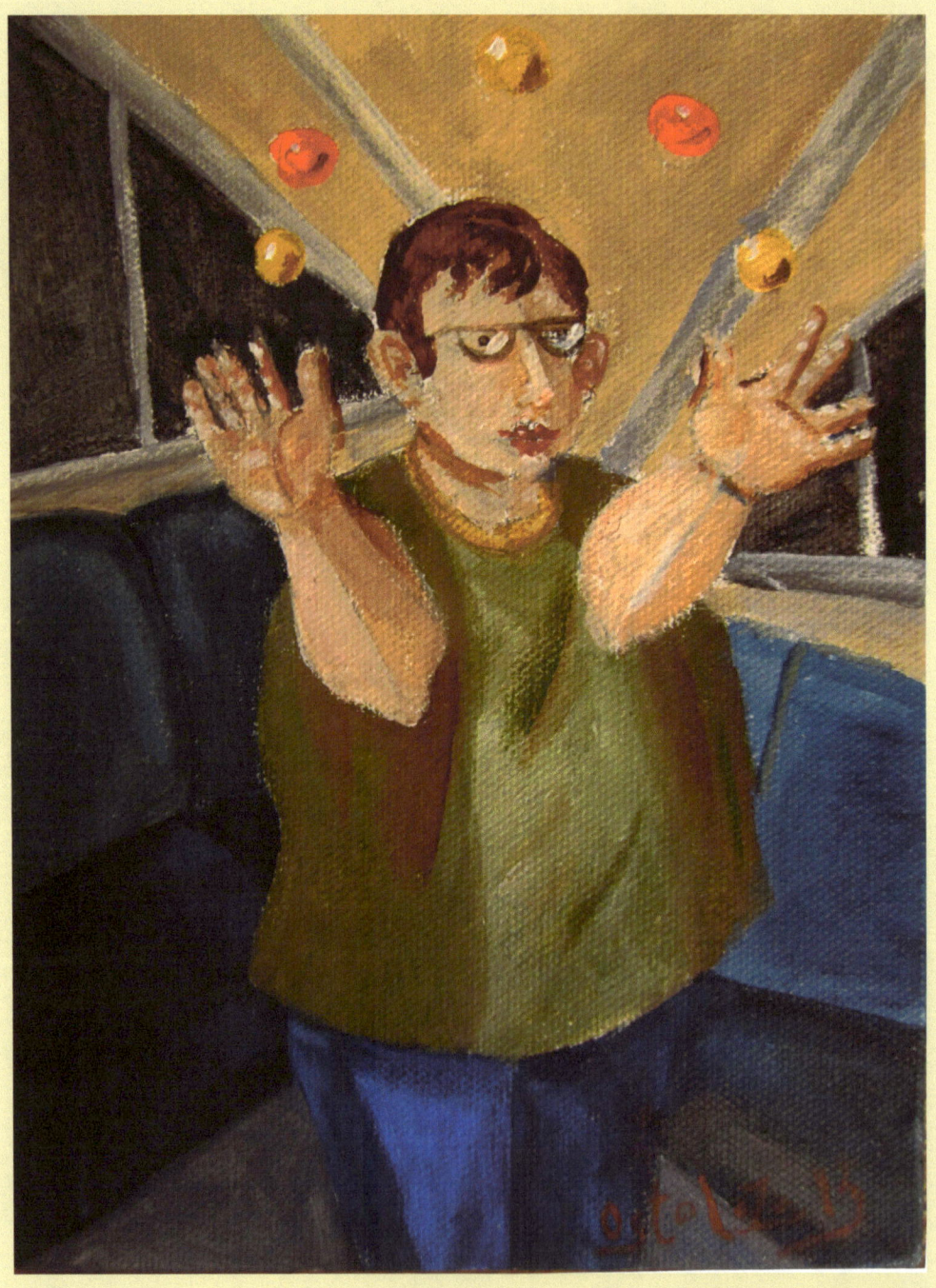

Acknowledgments

to Jonathan Aaberg, for believing in me as an artist, and whose
skills and dedication made possible the publication of this book;

to Audrey and John Kimball, and Grace von Perry,
for their friendship and support.
Thank you!!

www.ingramcontent.com/pod-product-compliance
Lightning Source LLC
Chambersburg PA
CBHW040324190526
45162CB00007B/71